THE PAIN

This book is due on the last date stamped below.
Failure to return books on the date due may result
in assessment of overdue fees.

APR 1 9 2006		
MAY 1 1 REC'D		
OCT 1 3 2006		
SEP 2 9 REC'D		
DEC 2 0 2012		
DEC 2 0 2012		
FINES	.50 per day	

This volume is made possible through grants from the National Endowment for the Arts (a federal agency), Andrew W. Mellon Foundation, the Lila Wallace-Reader's Digest Fund and the City of Houston through The Cultural Arts Council of Houston, Harris County.

Recovering the past, creating the future

Arte Público Press
University of Houston
Houston, Texas 77204-2090

Cover design by Mark Pinón

Najera, Rick.
    The pain of the macho / by Rick Najera.
      p.   cm.
    ISBN 1-55885-190-9 (alk. paper)
    1. Hispanic American men—Drama. 2. Masculinity
    (Psychology)—Drama. 3. Machismo—Drama. I. Title.
PS3564.A525P3   1997
812.54—dc21   96-39820
                                          CIP

CONTENTS

Pain of the Macho 7

Latinologues

    Monologues of the Latin Experience 53

A Quiet Love 93

Criticizing the Macho

"A macho force of one, highly exaggerated, slightly surreal and frequently funny, his one liners swing wildly from slapstick to barrio insight. On the heels of a cheap joke or an easy laugh he'll shift gears and turn serious with a vengeance."
—Sid Smith, *Chicago Tribune*

"There is humor, hope beneath this macho act. With genuine wit and social satire, Najera does not wallow in hurt but injects humor and nobility into seeming defeat. Najera is in control; a macho in search of meaning."
—Ernest Tucker, *Chicago Sun-Times*

"Pain of the Macho is a stinging ethnic satire... His writing acknowledges the tensions between Anglos, Latinos, men and women without rancor or malice."
—Holly Johnson, *Sacramento Bee*

"His writing is adept, wise and funny. His searing barbs cut to the heart of things and his unblinking honesty produces big laughs."
—Carmela Rago, *Chicago Reader*

FOR EDWARD NAJERA

SHOWTIME'S *"Latino Laugh Festival"* at Beethovan Hall, San Antonio, Texas.

Cast/Crew (*From left to right*):

Geraldo Rivera,
Erik Estrada,
Luis Avalos,
Rick Najera/(Writer, Director),
Edward James Olmos,
Christina Saralegui,
Liz Torres,
Aida Maris,
Tony Plana,
Paul Block,
Maria Concita Alonzo,
Jeff Valdez,
Rudy Moreno,
Sal Lopez,
Maty Mumford, and
Daisy Fuentes.

Photograph by: Al Rendin
Courtesy of Nan Leonard & Christina Saralegui June, 1996.

THE PAIN OF THE MACHO

FORWARD

The Pain of the Macho was first performed at The Good-man Theatre in Chicago on July 8, 1993 under the direction of John Bowab. The one-man show was performed and written by Rick Najera. It has since played in various theaters throughout the United States.

CAST & STAFF

Macho	**Rick Najera**
Director	**John Bowab**
Lighting Design	**T.J. Gerckens**
Sound Design	**David Naunton**
Stage Manager	**Leila Knox**

1. PROLOGUE

A radio plays Latin music, strong and sensual. Then the station fades to salsa sounds and finally to "Babalue." The radio sounds as though it is searching the Latin air waves. The lights on stage rise slowly to reveal a Day of the Dead altar that stands in the middle of the stage. It is decorated with costume pieces and pictures of various people who later we will meet. Among the pictures painted and photographed are those of a cholo, an I.N.S. agent, a busboy, an illegal alien and a beauty queen. It is a display of the living and the dead. In front of the altar, high in the rafters of the stage is a banner of a man in a matador pose, and underneath the banner the words "The Pain of the Macho" appear. Slowly, the stage, grows dark. In the darkness, we hear the music reach a crescendo, then the music stops. There is a beat, then quickly, a somber announcer's voice in the darkness is heard.

ANNOUNCER: Ladies and gentlemen, in this performance of The Pain of the Macho, the role of the Macho will not be performed by Rick Najera.

The banner is rolled up into the rafters. The altar starts to be moved off stage by the dresser / stagehand. The stage is empty. Over the loudspeakers, we hear other voices.

#1 VOICE: What? Oh, man. What is this?

ANNOUNCER: Ladies and gentlemen, the role of the macho normally played by Rick Najera will not be played by Rick Najera.

#1 VOICE: What is this shit?

#2 VOICE: Chuy, shhhh.

ANNOUNCER: I repeat, Rick Najera will not play a macho.

#1 VOICE: Oh, this is bullshit! Those Anglos get your hopes up, then they dash 'em! Let's riot like those Guatemalans did in L.A.!

ANNOUNCER: Rick Najera will not play a macho.

#2 VOICE: Let's get up early and use our lawn blowers on those Anglo bastards.

#1 VOICE: Estos cabrones, Shakespeare es mierda. ¡Mata a David Mamet! ¡Viva Lope de Vega! ¡Mata el Anglo Theater! ¡Ladrones! ¡Sinvergüenzas! Riot!

#2 VOICE: Riot! Riot!

ANNOUNCER: Please remain calm. God, these people are passionate.

#2 VOICE: Riot! Let's get our land back and our ticket money!

Sound effects of a full-blown riot start, i.e. glass breaking, people screaming and sounds of destruction. Rick Najera runs onto the empty stage. He is half-dressed and out of breath.

RICK: Please remain calm. Puerto Ricans stop inciting the Mexicans. Mexicans stop inciting the Puerto Ricans. Cubans stop inciting everybody. In the name of Edward James Olmos... *(The rioting sound effects stop immediately.)*

Thank you. I'm Rick Najera. I'm sorry, but I can't play a macho tonight. My therapist has warned me not to play a macho. He feels it would be very dangerous because I have worked very hard to get rid of the macho and I just don't want to regress. I hate the word macho. I prefer the more politically correct term: "Latino males with strong opinions." I have been in therapy to forget the macho inside of me. And it's working. I have learned to be less angry and not to blame shift. *(Yells.)*

"America stole my land!"—that's blame-shifting. I don't want to do that. I want to be a friendly minority that dances folklórico on Sundays.

Also, I'm learning to use non-confrontational vocabulary. I say things like, "You make me sad when you act so stupid."

I'm dealing with my macho nightmares. I started therapy because I wanted to understand them. Here's one of them: I'm running in a forest with a small six-inch spear and men with twelve-inch spears are running after me and I'm envious of them. I don't know what that means. That's one. The other happens when I'm on a camping trip and Michael Jackson is my scout leader. He says I have hyperthermia and if I don't get into a sleeping bag with him, I'll die. The third is a werewolf nightmare, but I'm bitten by a Chihuahua. Every full moon, I grow tan hair all over my body. I go ballistic and they find people with bite marks all over their heels.

Don't tell me I'm the only one who's had those nightmares. Oh, you do, too? *(He points to a guy in the audience.)*

Thank you. I would like to bond with you and I would hug you, but I'm still dealing with homophobia. Not that I am, but I'm worried about you!

How can I be a macho? I was never part of a street gang. I failed the written test. I didn't know what colors to wear 'cause I'm a winter. I was never in a drive by, but I was in a drive thru once. Does that count? I've never felt the pain of the barrio. Barrio, there's no pain there. Barrio just means neighborhood, just like "Mr. Rogers' Neighborhood." Except, we don't let old Anglo bachelors play with our children. That's an Anglo thing. Sorry, I don't mean to blame shift—what you people do is your business.

I don't want to play a macho! Macho. What does that word mean? See, a macho has no questions. A macho is self-assured. He has no doubts. But I have doubts, insecurities. What does the word macho mean? Words can mean so many things. If I say "apple," some of you may see a red apple and some of you may see a green apple, depending on your experiences with apples. Our experiences define the meanings of words.

If I say Latino, what do you see? Mexican American? Hispanic? What do you see? Macho, what do you see? If I say macho, you see a swaggering womanizer, a dark, cruel Latino. You'd see the "other," the "foreigner," the alien, "a macho."

When I say macho, I see my grandfather, a man: good, kind, gentle and strong. He was a macho. He raised fighting cocks. Anglos always say "ouch" when I say that. He raised fighting roosters. He was a macho. I can't forget him. *(The Day of the Dead altar is wheeled back on stage.)*

This is a "Day of the Dead" altar. We use it to remember the people who have left us. We put up their pictures and some of their favorite food and things by which we remember them.

Here's a picture of my grandfather. I asked my grandfather when he had crossed the border. "When I crossed there wasn't one," he said. There wasn't a border when he crossed. No borders. Now there's plenty of borders. What a thought, no borders?

Here is my grandfather's journal. This is the journal of the personal history of a macho. It is a large thick book. There are only two actual pages that are written on because machos never write anything down. They pass things down, *órale.* In it are recipes for cinnamon rolls and French bread.

He was a baker and a boxer. He loved to bake and fight. My therapist called him dysfunctional because he could hurt you or feed you. He always fed me. He had massive mitts for hands, but they were so gentle. As a child, I felt like a fragile creature beside him. I must have been so alien to him.

On the other pages, there are written strange names and birthdays—names I didn't recognize, names like Pepe Blanco, Pepe Rojo, Pepe Bizmo. They are the names and birthdays of his prized roosters that he loved to train. He had memorized the birthdays of his human family, but he couldn't memorize the birthdays of his roosters. A macho has a big heart. Forgive him if he can't memorize the birthdays of all the ones he loves.

I thought he would live forever, but he died in an old folks' home. I saw him before he died. A stroke had left him paralyzed—not very macho. He would have preferred a cattle stampede. His fighting hands couldn't beat time. He couldn't live forever. He died alone.

We were successful. We were Americanized. We didn't have to keep our machos with us. We could afford to keep him in an old folks home. That is a true story about a true macho.

This altar is here to help me remember, because the most fragile thing in the world is a memory. Sometimes, the most fragile thing is a macho. Words are full of contradictions. Aren't they?

For the memory of my grandfather, for him and all the other machos I've known, I will play the macho. I'll play a macho for just one night and, for just one night, I'll remember.

(Rick exits.)

ANNOUNCER: Ladies and gentleman the role of the macho will be played by Rick Najera.

VOICE #2: Oh, good, Chuy.

VOICE #1: Good, I hate to riot. I've got season tickets.

(Stage goes dark.)

BLACKOUT.

2. ALEJANDRO

A radio in the altar plays Latin music. The beat is primitive and earthy. The altar starts to open, splitting in half. A red light emanates from the altar.

The lights reveal Rick now in a tuxedo and standing in a matador's pose. Matador music plays. Roses are thrown to him. He looks around at the audience. He stands alone. Light silhouettes him. He wears a tuxedo jacket shaped like a matador with a large feathered serpent painted on the back. His back is to the audience. He yells a "grito." He gives a flower to a member of the audience. In a dramatic pose, he kneels, urging the audience to attack him as if it were a bull. Rick is now a toreador. He has now become the first macho of the evening, "Alejandro."

ALEJANDRO: I'm a macho. I'm a great macho. I am *the* macho... I fight the bulls. In my mind, I'm always fighting the bulls. But in real life, I'm fighting the INS. I'm fighting the deportation, the health department and the bad tippers. I've been gored twice by bad tippers!

I'm the macho, but I'm also the busboy. So if I can get you people anything, just let me know. Coffee, tea, water?

I take my work very *serio-sa-ly*. Oh, there may be jobs that may seem more important. But are they really? Sure, if you're a fireman and have a bad day, someone can get killed. If you're a busboy and have a bad day, someone can get hepatitis or food poisoning. Someone can get caffeinated instead of decaf. *(Alejandro finds a blonde woman.)*

Oh, you're beautiful! The busboys would love to serve you over and over again. Women love us busboys because we're mysterious. We fill up your cup and we're gone just like two ships passing in the night. We have our secrets and we leave no written record. We pass everything down. Orale! Latino men love women. We love to please them.

There are some Latinas who love women, too. They generally are bad tippers, but great tennis players.

Look at that beautiful woman. She's gorgeous. You're my favorite! The other one was just a fling. *(To the other girl.)* I'll call you. She's looking at me. She wants me. *(He walks over to center stage.)*

Ay, you are beautiful. The rest meant nothing. I've waited my whole life for you. Do you want me? Do you like us Latin lovers? You do want me. Oh, you want more coffee? All right, right away!

A macho must have more than one woman. I have two. One lives out of the country; one lives in the United States. I love them both. I just love my girlfriend closest to me more often.

Ay, blonde women, you are so beautiful! Us machos get extra macho points for dating blondes, which can lead to valuable coupons and wonderful prizes. A friend I knew dated a blonde. He got so many macho points and coupons that he got a barbecue set and World Cup final tickets. I knew another busboy who dated a famous blonde woman. I'm sworn to secrecy. But I can tell you that she dated Warren Beatty and is like a virgin, but far from one. If you're Catholic you can't say her name while making love.

You are so beautiful. You remind me of this Anglo woman I used to date. She was beautiful, like you. *(Beat.)* I guess dating is stretching it just a bit, but it was a very intense couple of hours. I remember meeting her at this fancy restaurant—fine wine, music. I was looking great in my tuxedo and I was feeling suave. She was my customer and I was her busboy.

I know how dangerous, how unprofessional... We in the food-service industry have a saying: "Never get sexually involved with your client. Leave that to trained psychiatric professionals or Supreme Court Justices."

She had a pierced nose. It wasn't a clip-on kind. It was a real pierced one. She wore it as a form of protest against the oppression of the Third World. Luckily, I was a member of the Third World.

Our eyes met after serving her half-caffeinated, half-decaf cappuccino. We really hit it off. She was sexy in that feminine sort of way. Actually, all she had to be was female to be sexy for me.

I had been giving her good service for most of the night. Now she wanted me. Why me? I wondered. Was she a food-service groupie, or maybe she had heard about my legendary rise from dishwasher to busboy in only three short years? Success is an aphrodisiac for women. However, one does not question good fortune or over-tipping.

Our hands met after I had served her some Sweet-N-Low. It was perfect. She was sweet. I was low. We looked into each other's eyes. She said, "Would you like to visit my performance art slash apartment space to see me perform?" So I say, "Sure, because I'm really interested in art, especially performance art." Then I say, "I'll get off work in one hour, or thirty minutes, ten, I quit."

I quit my job. I ran after her like the bulls from Pamplona. I ran after the dream. Well, I go there and she is all over me, kissing me and everything. It was like "The Postman Rings Twice," that classic film with Sharon Stone, Vanna White—all those white women look the same to me. I am filled with passion.

She tells me how much she loves my people, and I tell her how much I love it that she loves my people. She says she hates being Anglo. I say, "I hate you being Anglo, too." She says she hates conformity, and I say I hate conformity, too. She says she loves individuality, and I say I love individuality, too, especially since she does. She says she's independent. I say we could be independent together. She says that by talking to me she has learned so much about my people, and now she wants to learn more. I say, "Baby, I want to give you my big cultural lesson!"

She goes crazy. She says I am like an Aztec warrior and she is my slave, even though she is a feminist. And she is beautiful. We make mad, passionate love. I want to be with her and she with me. For one moment, our inhibitions are gone. We dance the forbidden dance, we do a naked Lambada. Each one of us is an ambassador for each other's tribe. Each other's curiosity is inflamed. Everything is inflamed.

She probes my secrets; I probe hers. She asks, "Is it true Latins are fantastic lovers?" I say, "It's true." She says, "Is it true Latino men can make love for hours without stopping?" I say, "Uh, uh uh, well... It's true, if it's not tax time or I'm not having immigration trouble or the "Big Spin" isn't on television. It's true." She says, "Is it true Latino men are hung like bulls?" I say, "Who's been telling you this stuff, Cubans?"

I ask her, "Is it true Anglos run most major national corporations in America?" She says, "It's true." I ask her, "Is it true that father knows best?" She says, "It's true." I say, "Is it true the CIA and FBI conspired to assassinate Kennedy?" She says, "It's true." Wow, she knows everything. She's like Oliver Stone, but with breasts.

Oh, I could marry her and be a part of the American Dream, buy a citizenship through copulation. I reach for my fiesta-colored condom. Then she hands me her own condoms. She has twenty-four different brands. She even has a brand with her picture on the box. She knows what consumer reports say about each one.

She has satin sheets. She is shameless. She knows what she's doing. I start to get scared. She grabs me in a headlock. I say, "Be gentle!" I look under her bed for ice picks because I saw that movie "Basic Instinct." She pins me over and over again. She is a real sports fan. Oh, I want her! Oh, I want to invade her. Conquer her. Take her. Possess her! *(Sings.)* I want to live in A-A-mer-i-ca! Ok by me in A-mer-i-ca!

Well, we make love all night long. *(Screams in orgasmic pain.)* It is wonderful. Then, the most marvelous thing happens. We see the sunrise holding each other like Adam and Eve in the New World. She is not Anglo, she's an angel. I am not a Latin lover, I'm just her lover. I am the one who cherishes and loves her; yes, LOVE. I said the word. I committed to that word. Because in this lonely world, love does matter. You can sometimes hold it and, for a brief second, I held her and I held love.

I am not Latino or even a man. I am just two dark eyes that she says she loved. Two dark eyes for her to look into, two dark eyes attached to a face, a body and a soul.

Well, the next morning I get up early, make her an omelet. I make her breakfast in bed. I clean her house. I want to snuggle and talk about what happened last night. She says I talk too much and lights a cigarette. I say, sure, baby. *(Sings.)* "Oh my woman I love her so, she'll never know." She says she has to go. I say I want her to meet my mother and learn to make those corn tortillas I love so much. She says she'll call me. She says she'll call *me!*

She puts my uniform outside the hall. I get dressed there. She must have been in a hurry. I hear her behind the door saying that she'll call me. Well, I don't wait for her. The next day, I call her over and over again. Finally, she returns my call. And, with that beautiful voice, devoid of any trace of accent, she says, "I can't see you, Alejandro. I want you to know that I had a wonderful time, but I can't see you anymore." Oh, before she hangs up she says, "I hope this does not add to your feelings of abandonment." I say, "Not at all." But she is already gone.

Sometimes a macho wounds and sometimes he is wounded. More coffee on table three, right away! And some Sweet-N-Low to that woman who should have got it fifty pounds ago. More coffee right away!

Slow Guy flashes his gang signs. Then we hear gunshots and a car screeching away. The stage goes to darkness as we hear Slow Guy crumbling to the floor.

3. SLOW GUY

In the darkness, Rick quickly changes from Alejandro to his next macho. He starts to shuffle. The lights rise as Kid Frost's "It's a Thin Line" plays. Rick is now dressed in a gang jacket and an L.A. Raiders cap. He is Slow Guy. He shuffles slowly from years of glue sniffing. He "tags" a wall and sniffs the paint rag. He moves to the music rhythmically and sometimes out of sync. He is in his own world, dancing to a different beat with his arrogant cholo pride.

SLOW GUY: My name is Slow Guy because... *(Stops.)* I'm getting paged. Excuse me, some negocios. *(He pulls a cellular phone from his jacket and talks.)*

Yeah, O.K. I said I can get you two kilos later, not now. I can get you that. No. What do you mean? I'll get it when I get it. Don't threaten me. Don't... Hey, I'll kill you! I'll get it when I get it. Don't threaten to kill me. I'll... O.K., O.K., O.K. Two kilos rice and beans. All right. I love you, too, mom. *(He puts away the phone.)*

My name is Slow Guy because, because, because... I don't know why they call me Slow Guy. Alejandro, the guy who works at the restaurant, he says Slow Guy's a bad name to have if you're looking for a job. A better name is Work Hard Guy, Minimum Wage Guy, Kiss Your Anglo Butt and Work Cheap Guy.

Alejandro says I've been in this country for two generations and I'm still a dishwasher. He says after two generations here and the American school system, I should be more than a dishwasher. I should be a busboy!

Yeah, he says Slow Guy is a bad name to have. But I ain't going to change my name. It's my name. It's my placa. I put up my placa all over town, on Avenue 42nd, my placa's there, with all my homeys. You can see it from here. *(Reads.)*

Chato, Little Chato, Sad Girl, Boxer, uh, uh, Little Man, Dopey, Happy, Sleepy, Sneezy, Bashful, Grumpy, Doc. I wanted to be famous like Chaka. His name is everywhere. He's famous.

Well, I am going to be famous. This famous guy, he's an artist, he said we're all going to be famous for fifteen minutes. His name is... I forget. Don't tell me. I ain't no glue sniffer. His name is... Do you know it? *(Listens.)* Andy Warhol? No, his name is Luis Alfaro. He lives in my 'hood. He's real famous. He said everyone is going to be famous for fifteen minutes. He thought that up, *¿sabes qué?* He uses his head. I am going to get my fifteen minutes of fame. I am going to be a movie star, a super *estrella*—or at least a working extra.

I have already done three films as an extra. I was in "Colors," "Mi Vida Loca" and "Ghetto Blaster." 'Cause, like, these companies come into my barrio with all these cops and food wagons and *gabachos* with walkie-talkies.

My homey, "Little Man" starts directing traffic and they pay him and I watch them film. There are these Filipino guys playing *cholos*; yeah, Filipino guys and one tan Anglo. And I say, "Hey, they ain't no gang guys, I am." And I show 'em my tattoos, and they say, "Hey, those look good. Let's put him in." Then I'm in the distance getting fifty bucks and Sean Penn's busting me, and I'm like famous for one minute.

And I meet all these famous people. I met Edward James Olmos during "Stand and Deliver." He's a saint. He cleaned up L.A. I came down to help Eddie. I thought it's good to help clean up. Besides, I might have forgotten something or dropped something during the riots. I'm still trying to find that left shoe. I dropped it near a Payless Shoe Store. Eddie's famous, and I'm going to be famous

and they will take my picture. It won't be front, then pro-
file-type pictures. *(He mimes getting a mug shot.)* It'll be
my picture smiling and shit. I'll let 'em. The Indians didn't
let no Anglos take their pictures because they were worried you would steal their souls. But I want them to take
my picture, to take my soul, and to be famous 'cause then
I'll be up in the movies. In the movies, your soul's safe.
You live forever. Not here on the street, you don't live
long.

I'm doing lots of gang and Latino crime films now.
There's going to be plenty of work for Chicano extras. Hollywood needs us. Hollywood loves to exploit, I mean
employ us Latinos. There will be lots of work for me,
'cause I know how to be an extra. I was an extra at home,
an extra at school and an extra in the neighborhood. I've
been an extra all my life.

I'm working all the time. I was on "911" once as a victim. I had a hernia during the riots. I didn't lift with my
legs. I lifted with my back. I got a sofa, but my mother
said it didn't match the living room set she just got, so she
made me take it back.

I was on "Cops" once as a perpetrator and once as a
victim. I was the guy being chewed up by the Doberman. I
do my own stunts. I was on "America's Most Wanted"
once as an actor, twice as an actual criminal.

I got a lot more time left. I know how to be an extra.
We all do, and the camera loves us. The camera captures
our souls. I got a few minutes more of fame, *¿sabes qué?*
They pay me forty bucks for the day and then it's over.
They leave, but I'm still here. I live here in the real barrio
and my home boys really get killed here and that ain't no
movie. I'm the real thing. They better be back soon. They
better pick me up 'cause they dropped me off in the wrong
'hood. *(He looks around, desperately searching for land-
marks.)* This ain't my barrio. This is White Fence not

Frog Town. I'M IN THE WRONG 'HOOD! They dropped me off in the wrong 'hood!

I'll be all right. I got fourteen minutes of fame I've used up. I've got one minute of fame left. I got to just stay proud. *Con safos, ese.*

They're supposed to have dropped me off in my barrio, not here. I've got to get out of here. Last time they did this, some gang guys came up to me, mad-dogging me. They said, "You got a face tha's up to no good, *ese.*" I said, "Hey, don't give me no *pedo*... I'm making a movie." They said, "Where's the camera?" And I said, "It's coming." Then the cops came up and they said, "Hey, what are you doing here?" I said, "I'm making a movie." And they said, "Where's the camera?" I said, "It's coming, I think."

They dropped me off here like Kevin Costner in "Dances with Wolves." But I feel more like "The Last of the Mexihicans." The transport guy, he don't like me because I used Erik Estrada's trailer. Well, I had to go, and Erik and I are homeboys. He invited me to his house for dinner. I said, "Erik, where's the rap party?" So he gave me directions, but he left off some numbers... and the actual city... He's under a lot of pressure. He forgets. This is his comeback film.

Oh man, homey, those *vatos* are coming back again. They're mad-doggin' me. I ain't scared. I fight crazy. I'm crazy. I wish I was up in the movies right now. The Indians didn't let you take pictures of them because they were worried you'd steal their souls. I say take mine. Take my soul. I'll be safe up there. *¿Sabes qué?* I'm the real thing. That transport guy better remember to pick me up. They'll come back. I've got nothing to worry about. They need me. I'm the real thing. I got one more minute of fame left. Nothing can happen to me. I'm making a movie. I'm making a movie! I'm making a movie. *(Sound effects.)*

Gunshot... BLACKOUT.

4. DESI

"Babalú" music plays. Slides of Desi flash on a screen behind him. Then a picture of Desilu Studios in its old glamour appears. In the dim light, we see Rick's dresser pull off Slow Guy's jacket and cap and put on him a fifties' dinner jacket. Rick has now become Desi Arnaz. He has a 1940s style microphone in his hand. There are silhouettes of palm trees and a conga. The light hits Desi in the face. He starts to do his famous Desi laugh.

DESI: Lucy, I'm home, heh heh heh! *(Laughs.)* Hey, Babalú... Babalú! Heh, heh, heh! Oh, thank you, Miami Rotary Club. It's great to be here with all you Cuban Young Republicans and receive this award tonight, the Best Latino on Television Award 1954. *(Applause sound effects are heard.)*

Wow, I'm the only Latino in television, but that's O.K. I have received many awards, the Mexican of Togetherness Award, the M.O.T.A. Most recently, I have been invited to Georgia to receive the Latino Young National Couple Humanist award, the L.Y.N.C.H. award, for my marriage to Lucy. *(He laughs.)*

"Hey, Babalú!" Does anyone in America know what those words mean? It's Indian, not Spanish. I'll translate. It's Indian for 'Get back on the Mayflower, Pilgrim!' They almost gave me the L.Y.N.C.H. award in Texas for that joke.

The future is going to be great for us Latinos. In the future, there will be thousands of movies about us on the air. There has to be; there's millions of us. When I first told the network about my idea for the show, they said for me to be Lucy's husband was not a good idea. How about a white guy? I could be the gardener. I said, "I've been married to her for twelve years." They said, "O.K., let's give it a try." And it worked.

Then they said "We want the rerun rights." I said "Are you sure?" and they said, "Desi, people pay for and want to see new shows, not old reruns." I hung on to the rerun rights, even though they offered me beads and mirrors and blankets. They said it had worked the last time.

Normally, that stuff works, but I believed in Lucy and I believed in this country. I came here, not a penny in my pockets. I cleaned bird cages. I love this country. America doesn't just belong to the first guys off the Mayflower, but the last guys off the boat, even if it's a banana boat. Heh! heh! heh! Life's looking up for Latinos, and it's going to get better. They say, "Desi, you just keep them laughing at you!" "You be the funny guy," I say. I would like to play better roles. Tyrone Power does "Blood and Sand." Why can't I? They say, "Desi, be cute, not sexy. Be safe, not dangerous. Let *us* worry about image." I say O.K. You guys have been doing a great job so far. *¡Ay coño!*

There's going to be a lot of shows about Latinos. They asked me if I had any ideas. So I told the networks about some ideas of mine for new shows with Latino themes. I said, "Well, I got one about this Latino family in Texas. It's about some Mexican guy. He's hunting in Texas. He shoots into the ground and up comes some bubbling crude, gold that is, Texas tea. Everyone says, 'José, move away from there. Beverly Hills is the place you ought to be.' So they write it down.

They say, "Desi, have you got more ideas?" So I say, "Well, I got another one about some Cubans in a boat on a two-hour tour. Their boat gets blown onto an island off Haiti. They can't get off the island. Can you imagine Cubans who cannot get off an island? I got a Batista millionaire and a movie star from the Copa Cabana. It's going to be great! There's also this Navy guy and his little buddy Gilberto. They have a unique relationship, totally platonic. It's wacky. I call it 'Gilberto's Island'."

They say, "Desi, do you have other ideas?" I say, "Well, I got another show I call 'Bewitched'; about a Santería witch from the Dominican Republic married to an advertising executive. There's chicken heads on the floor... It's wacky."

Then the network guys say, "Give us one more!" I say "O.K., this is my favorite show. It's about a guy in a white Panamanian suit and this kinky midget who dresses in Corinthian leather. He lives on an island and provides adults with their fantasies, much like a Puerto Rican pimp I knew in *Nueva York*.

The guys in the network say, "Desi, these ideas will never work." Those guys were really looking out for me. They said, "Desi, you keep them laughing." Well, I'm laughing. Heh, heh, heh.

I invented the three-camera sitcom. I created an industry. I'm no clown. I'm laughing all the way to the bank. I've made it. Lucy and I got everything we want. More people watch our show at night than the President's inauguration. I got the "Best Latino on Television" award. Well, I'm still the only Latino on television, but there will be thousands some day. This is some sort of dream. If Lucy was here, she would tell you America is a candy store for her Desi. She is the mother of my children and I love Lucy. She can't make it tonight, but you still want me. Don't you?

You still love me, eh? Everyone in America loves Lucy and me. And Lucy loves me. I get very lonely on the road, Lucy. I want so much. *(Sings.)*

"I love Lucy and she loves me. We're as happy as two can be. Sometimes we quarrel now and then. Oh, how we love to make up again. No one kisses like Lucy can. She's my misses and I'm her man and life is heaven you see. Because I love Lucy and she loves me..."

You've got to dream big. Hey, Lucy, she always is crying 'cause she wants to be in the show. *(He calls off to a man off stage.)*

Tony, try to get her back on the phone. Why won't she talk to me? I don't understand. We wanted this show; we got what we wanted. *(He starts to break down.)*

Ay coño, that girl.

Beat. He looks at the audience and stops. He realizes he has revealed too much and goes back to his public persona.

That girl, ay, that girl, that girl... Hey, Lucy, I just got another idea for a show. *(He starts to sing "Babalú" as lights fade.*

FADE OUT.

5. MACHO 101

Off stage, Rick has changed quickly from Desi into Doctor Steve Sánchez. The lights come up on Doctor Steve Sánchez, an old gravely-voiced Chicano Studies professor. He's dressed in a white lab coat and holds some books at the podium. Through his horn-rimmed glasses, he peers at the audience, which has now become his class. A class bell rings.

DR. STEVE SÁNCHEZ: Everyone just sit down and get ready for class. I am Professor Steve Sánchez and this is Macho 101. I am an expert on the macho. I got my doctorate at Mannie's House of Family counseling, Mannie's Number 6 in East Los Angeles, where you can get a free *chimichanga* with every psychiatric session.

I know the macho well and so can you. There is nothing more exciting than watching a macho running free in the wild or just cruising at the Red Onion. You, too, will know a macho.

To properly study the macho, you'll need to sign up for a few courses. Also, there is the macho-watching field trip to Standard Brands Paint Store. Very exciting! Pass that around. *(He passes around a sign-up sheet.)*

You'll also sign up for the Hairy Man Weekend in Tijuana. Give that to your hairy man. You'll need this book, "Iron Juan," by Dr. Steve Sánchez, just $29.95. It's mandatory reading. *(Points to woman.)*

You can be my teacher's aide. Pass this announcement around: "The truck and tractor couples retreat has been moved to Valentine's Day."

I hear you whispering among yourselves. Well, I'd like to say that I was not at the girls' dorm last night, a nasty rumor started by a Women's Studies professor. She's a lesbian. I know this because she didn't want me. Any woman that doesn't want me must be a lesbian. You'll be surprised how many lesbians are out there.

Now, some of you here are actually married to machos. Let's see a show of some hands. Hmm, you haven't been trained very well at all. How many men are married to *machacas?* Let's see those hands. Well, you've been trained much better. You know, *machaca* comes from the Spanish word *machacar.* Repeat after me. *Machacar.* Very Good. *Machacar* means "to shred the beef" and if you're married to a *machaca* you've had your beef shredded many times.

Now, some of you might be mistresses to a macho and that's why you're taking this course. I know who you are because I see the red Mazda Miatas in the parking lot.

I want to talk to you about the Hairy Man Weekend in Tijuana. You must take precautions, especially you women and some effeminate men.

Now, you need to carry this with you, which you can buy for $17.95 at the back of the room. This device will scare off any macho. *(He shows slide rule.)* You will use it as follows: flash it to the attacker and say: "This is your reality check. Yours is not 10 inches. Back! Back!"

Machos come in various forms and types. For instance, there's Anglo machos. The difference between an Anglo macho and a Latino macho is that Anglo machos usually attack in large groups after U.N. approval. Latino machos attack whenever they damn well please, especially after a World Cup Soccer game.

There are also Black machos. If you're wondering if you are a Black macho, ask yourself this. In the Ike and Tina movie did you jump up and say *(In Black dialect.)* "Hey, how about Ike, Tina? He made you, girl!" If you side with Ike, then you may be a black macho. There are also Asian machos. They lie about the size... of their properties. *(In Asian dialect.)* "Twelve stories, fully erect!"

There's also animal machos. The lion, for instance, is one. The lioness hunts for the lion while he lounges about doing absolutely nothing. However, when the lion mates, he can mate up to twelve hours at a time. And if any man here can do that, I bet your woman will put on some Lee Press on Nails and drag a wilderbeast home to your lazy ass any day of the week.

But let's begin by defining the word macho. What does the word macho mean? Is it an antiquated term that my ex-wife used at my custody hearings? "I'm a fit father, I say!" *(Catches himself.)* Perhaps, I'm revealing too much.

Can there be good machos? Yes, the Knights of the Round Table, men of action, kind machos, protectors.

Is a patriarchal society a necessary evil? Are people born with an extra macho chromosome? I don't know. You tell me. They don't pay me enough to know everything. Besides, I was out last night drinking heavily, doing research on macho mating rituals, so I could not prepare for this lecture. I do know this, the macho comes in two forms: Good and bad, yin and yang, Rush Limbaugh and Phil Donahue. We must embrace and accept our savage macho selves and control our wild and destructive macho selves. Luckily, I'm in control and I've tamed the macho within me.

To study the macho properly, I must trace his history. The beginning of the macho can be traced back to Spain, *Ethpaña*. Repeat after me, *Ethpaña*. They have a lisp. That is why they overcompensate: they have to prove themselves. They invented cockfighting in 1200 A.D. Now, man invented it by putting horrible sharp spurs in the little feet of roosters. Later, he tried it with French poodles and it wasn't very successful.

The next macho took place in Mexico: Hernando Cortez. He said the largest macho lie yet: "We don't want gold. We're just tourists. Moctezuma, show us the way to Ixtapa!"

Now understand this: machos will lie to you sometimes to get what they want. I see this on so many street corners. *(Holds up sign.)* "Will give commitment for sex."

Machos will never give commitment for sex, unless it's really good sex. Commitment to a macho is normally about an hour, depending on whether there's a football game on TV or not.

But before we go on, let's address some macho business; as good machos are organized. First, I want to know who's going to lead the Hairy Man weekend course in Tijuana? Fight among yourselves and decide who will lead the course. Also, who's going to the truck and tractor pull to study the macho up close? Be careful, no sudden movements or hard concepts or big words. You might enrage one.

You. *(Points to a beautiful woman.)* I have a special assignment. I want you to go home and fill my Jacuzzi with lime green jello and wait for me. I'll be there right away. We'll see if machos can breed in captivity. I'm sorry. That was very unprofessional. *(Whips himself.)* That was the dark macho. I'm in control now.

Be careful of the dark machos, ladies. To him, there are only two kinds of women: virgins like his mother or Madonna, who is like a virgin. Always appeal to the higher macho in him, his good macho, and maybe they will believe you at the Senate sexual harassment hearing. Or they might believe you at the next faculty review board meeting, where you will try to get my tenure revoked. I'm innocent! I didn't know she was a student!

Sorry, where was I?

Us machos have a difficult time relating to women. This adds to our existential loneliness, or in layman's terms, why we can't get laid on a Saturday night. Women want love first, before sex. We want sex so that we may feel love. We both want the same thing. The trouble is the order in which we want them. However, both sexes fear one thing: old age. Machos fear decay. We fear age, but I don't, 'cause I'm in control.

I was once desirable, when Nixon was president. Now I can't keep my toupee up. Last time I got laid, disco was in. I don't want to grow old and alone. And maybe in a young co-ed's arms, I will become young again and less lonely. But now, they see me as an old fool. All I want to say is that I'm in control. I'm in control of your grade. If you want an A for some T&A, I'm the guy! Forget this old, kind professor stuff. The hell with it! I'm an animal. My baser side won and he wants to get down. He wants to party, he wants to boogie-woogie-oogie. I'm cro-macho-man and I'm not extinct. *(Stunned.)* Oh no, the dark macho's out. I need to shave. He's returning. Run away. Class dismissed. There goes my tenure! Run away!

BLACKOUT.

6. MISS EAST L.A.

The class bell rings. As the slow dream-like music from "Evita" plays, Rick changes from his professor smock to a dress, a bouffant wig and hooped earrings. As the stage grows light, we see Rick tentatively and demurely walking on stage. The spotlight hits the beauty queen. Now transforming in front of the audience, first bouffant wig and tiara are adjusted, then a bouquet of roses is added. The final accessory that's added is a sash that says "Miss East Los Angeles" with ribbons attached that reveal her sponsors: Manteca Lard and JC Penney. She's stunned. Then tears fill Miss East L.A.'s eyes.

V. O.: Ladies and gentlemen, please give applause of appreciation to Miss East L.A., as she takes her final walk before she gives up her crown to one of these lucky girls. Miss East L.A. is sponsored by JC Penney, Manteca Lard and

Rosarita Refried Beans. *(Singing first in English, then in Spanish.)*

"Here she comes, Miss East L.A."

MISS EAST L.A.: *(Miss East L.A. stops and waves at the crowd.)* I have so many wonderful memories of my reign as Miss East L.A. What a wonderful year! The many *quinceañeras* I attended to give those little girls and their fathers hope. After spending as much on their little girls' coming-out party as on their mortgage—glamour was worth it.

One day, maybe, she would grow up to be Miss East L.A. That is, if their little girl would leave alone the sweet tamales and go easy on the guacamole and take beauty makeup lessons at JC Penney, like I did.

I want to thank JC Penney, who sponsored me for this event. Thank you. Also, I want to thank your Regional Manager, Burt Williams. When it comes to contests and pretty young girls, Burt said I was the contestant he most wanted to enter. Burt, as you reminded me, without you, I could not have made it. Thank you for sponsoring me, over and over again...

So many wonderful memories. I have been honored to lead my people as Miss East L.A. I am so happy. *(She sings to the tune from "Evita," "Don't Cry for me Argentina.")* "Don't cry for me, East L.A. I never forgot you. Not in my wild days in Montebello, which were only rumors spread by Chata Gonzales' mother, who tried to get me killed so her little fat girl could win my crown." *(She turns around and looks at the throne.)*

Now, I must give up my crown to one of these contenders for Miss East L.A., a contest which my family has controlled for so many years, including all my sisters, my mother and my legendary grandmother, María Noriega de Pinochet de Evita Los Angeles Gómez, who founded the Miss East L.A. contest. And now I must transfer my crown, my power, after only one short year.

Well, I don't think so. Do you think I would give up my crown this easily? Give up my scholarship to ITT Tech so easily? Where I will learn an exciting career as a nurse's assistant? No fucking chance. *(She pulls out a gun from her bouquet of roses and swings it about wildly.)*

Guards, seize them! Lock the doors. Princesses, follow me!

The military is in control. I have exposed the plot to force me to give up my crown and I am not going to give up my crown to one of these no-talent runner-uppers, these baton-twirling wannabe bitches from Pico Rivera! I've worked too hard! All those boring *folklórico* lessons! All those endless luncheons with sleazy politicians. Bill never called me back after he toured L.A. He didn't invite me to the inauguration. He promised me First Girlfriend. We could have looked cool cruising in Washington. I liposucked and plucked my body into this unnatural shape. *(Angrily.)*

JUST FOR MEN. BUT NO MORE MISS NICE GIRL! ALL RIGHT, NOBODY MOVES!!!

My princesses will form a *junta* with me as the leader and ruler, along with the help of my multinational corporation, JC Penney, and my American advisor, Burt Williams, a good friend to Oliver North. With the aid of the CIA, we will establish my reign over East L.A. I promise free elections as soon as this communist, left-wing attempted coup has been thwarted and my crown is secure. Then, after the people learn to vote correctly in a one-party system, a system I control, then there will be free elections for Miss East L.A.

I want Princess Debbie Noriega and Princess Gloria Pinochet from Pico Rivera arrested. They have plotted with Mary Kay and Jenny Gonzales against me.

I want the newspapers shut down, especially the ones that don't cover this event. Also, I want the Editor of *Low Rider Magazine*, who took that unflattering picture of me

in a one-piece bathing suit after I had some water reten-
tion and my *panza* was sticking out; I want him to be
taken out and shot. And people... nobody needs to get
hurt.

Did you think I would give up my crown this easily?
Never! *(She hisses as though she is possessed.)* But, please
don't worry. My reign will be glamorous and beautiful...
Unless the people don't obey me. Don't fuck with Miss
East L.A.! That could get ugly.

Free liposuction for the fat ones, free purple eye
shadow for the *cholas*, big hoop earrings for the Puerto
Rican cha cha queens, spandex bike pants for the Dominicans! Jenny Craig reduced calorie nachos for everyone!
*(Miss East L.A. trails off as we hear the "Evita" music
swell.)*

FADE TO:

7. CAPTURED BY FEMINISTAS

*Then we hear a jail door creaking open and slamming
shut. A man wrestles in the darkness with his captors. Rick
has now dressed back into Alejandro's busboy uniform. Rick is
now Alejandro. Alejandro is thrown on stage. The lights simulate jail bars all around him, seeming like a scene from some
bad Third-World prison drama. Alejandro's hands are tied
and he is blindfolded. He is thrown into the room.*

ALEJANDRO: Who are you? Why have you done this to me?
At least take off my blindfold. *(He takes off his blindfold
and looks into the audience, stunned.)* Oh, no! FEMI-
NISTAS! What I've always suspected from day one. A
feminista conspiracy, directed toward this macho. Well,

you bitches finally got me! *(A slapping sound is heard. He mimes being hit.)*

OW! Okay, you girls... *(Slap is heard.)* OOWW! Okay, you women... *(Slap is heard.)* OOWW! Okay, you self-actualized feminine goddesses who run with wolves. You finally captured me!

Well, you must feel pretty smug in your Birkenstocks, all looking at me. Gloria Steinhem, of course. Martina Navratilova, what took you so long? Oh, no, I knew it. Phil Donahue! You make me sick, always sucking up to the women. So, what are you all going to do. Kill me? Or maybe?

VOICE: *(A voice over is heard like a chant from the cultural revolution or a deprogramming tape.*

All men started off as women until their Y chromosome screwed up. You are mutants, return to your feminine good side. Women are able to communicate. Men are bad.

ALEJANDRO: Mind control, I knew it. Well, it won't work. I'm too stupid. So what's next? Are you going to shoot me? Well, you got me. What are you going to do, kill me? Go ahead. I'll show you how a macho man dies. I'll show you, I'll... *(Sound effects of a rifle bolt cocking back and drums for an execution are heard.)*

You're really serious? I'll show you. Go ahead, shoot me. But before you do, I've got one thing to ask. *(He breaks down into quivering male Jello.)*

Oh, please don't kill me! Please! *¡Por favor!* It will just take a second. Let me explain.

I know what the women have said about me. I know the charges. I never once said that Anita Hill lied; that's a rumor. I said Judge Mandingo lied. I was totally behind Anita. I like Jodi Foster films very much. I loved "Thelma and Louise" and "Go Fish." I've always supported day care, because I had a lot of children. You know, when you get out and party a lot like I do, day care is very important.

Hillary Clinton makes a wonderful president. As for the toilet-seat controversy, up or down, who cares? I'll go outside. Who needs to use a toilet? I'm a dog.

As for the woman's-right-to-choose movement, the whole right to life and that sort of thing... Listen, whatever you women would like is okay by me. Personally, I don't consider the fetus a fully formed human being until it can drive. So up until sixteen, it's fair game. Am I winning you over? Wait, put down the guns.

I think women are the most beautiful creatures in all God's kingdom. Maybe that was the problem.

Martina Navratilova, Gloria Steinhem, all you women, have mercy on me. Before you kill me, let me just say one thing! *(Desperate scream.)*

A woman raised me! *(The drum roll stops.)*

That's right! A woman gave me birth. It was a woman who said, "Big boys don't cry. Act like a man! Be tough!" It was a woman who gave me my first G.I. Joe set, my first little cowboy outfit and pistol. It was a woman who hit me. My mother had the cutest little mustache and the sneakiest right hook. It was a woman who did all these things to me.

A woman raised me, held me, taught me everything I know. Could I help but love them so much? Too much? I wanted to be with all women, over and over and over again. I wanted to return to the womb. It was a mother's love that trained me. Gloria Steinhem, I see I am getting to you.

Maybe we all have not been able to communicate well because of the inherent differences between the male and the female species... such as a man's inherent need for love and acceptance through sex, and a woman's inherent need for denying me sex ...even after I bought her a happy meal. Two things, opposed to each other in a dichotomy of failed relationships, you might say. So what I'm saying is maybe I've learned from this thing, too.

I could be reformed... I could learn to... *(He stutters.)* ... *cuddle* after sex. I could learn to communicate, to listen.

If I have ever offended women, forgive me. Their love spurred me on. It was because of a woman that I came onto this earth and I guess now the reason why I leave it. Go ahead, shoot me. That is, if your conscience lets you after looking into my doe-like eyes. Go head, shoot me! *(He prepares for the shot and realizes that it is not coming.)*

Gloria, I see that I have gotten through to you in a certain way. Maybe we all have learned from this tragic experience. Yet, if we tried, each one, men and women, to communicate in a better fashion, then this violence and bloodshed could be averted. Perhaps I could learn to cuddle after sex and to talk. *(Building in intensity.)* Well, maybe at least cuddle. Maybe I could learn to listen and to be sensitive. Maybe I could learn to cry, not just when I'm denied my way. Maybe I could show more emotion. I could learn to be more considerate in bed or in the car, wherever we do the wild thing.

Perhaps mankind, no forgive me, humans, humankind, no, not humankind, *womankind* will get along. I'll spell women with a "y," womyn. Who needs the men? And perhaps we could realize we are all brothers and sisters deep down, which is the most important thing. *(His hands are untied.)*

Thank you. Thank you. How kind of you to let me go. Okay. Now then, I just need a ride home. I was wondering if Gloria Steinhem or you could give me a ride home?

I'm so tense from this experience, I sure could use a Jacuzzi. You got one at your house? Good, maybe we could crack open a bottle of wine and just hang out together and talk. Maybe you can give me a massage and

I can give you a massage. It would be so nice. Gloria, for an old girl, you're looking good, baby. Maybe we could hang out. I could give you some gentle breast rolfing, and uncover some forgotten memories. Women hold a lot of tension in their inner thighs. *(Drum rolls of a firing squad starts again.)*

What's with the guns again? Hey! What did I say? I thought we were communicating?

BLACKOUT.

8. BUFFORD GOMEZ

The drum roll stops. The song "Shotgun" plays loud then fades. A projector on the back wall shows various super eight movies of the border: barbed wire, helicopters patrolling for illegal aliens, a border-patrol station, a roadblock, some highway workers with red California highway maintenance bags and reflector vests. Rick appears dressed as "Fidel," an illegal alien with cowboy boots, belt buckle and cowboy hat. Next, we see him in California maintenance gear, walking by the Border Patrol. The music swells and we see him running by a sign that says "Watch for Pedestrians Crossing the Freeway." An announcer talks about the number to call to report illegal aliens. The lights are seen reflecting from the city, the "city of the lights," Los Angeles. A blast from a highway crash is heard. We hear highway sounds. It's deafening. A car screeches. Then silence. Highway sound effects. Lights change. Rick has now changed into an I.N.S. Officer, Bufford Gómez. A car light catches him as he walks on stage. He speaks with a heavy Texas drawl and holds up a stop sign. He wears aviator glasses and looks menacing at first.

BUFFORD GÓMEZ: Yeah, America's number one! Number one! Grenada, Kuwait, Iraq, I have seen the world. Panama, South Central, I have seen the world. I've been "All I can be" in a lot of countries that didn't want me to be all I could be. This is a great country. Why would so many people try to come here if it wasn't?

My name is Bufford Gómez and I'm Mexican American, more American than Mexican, some might say. Well, I say to them, who asked you? I love this country. I've been decorated. Mexican Americans are the most decorated minority in America because we are given the opportunity to be the first to get drafted, the first in battle and the first to die. God Bless America!

We're always in the first wave. The first wave of soldiers in any war is always Blacks, Mexicans and a few hair stylists from San Francisco. Don't believe what you read. The military would love to put gays and minorities in any war zone, 'cause they want to give us the opportunity to die for this great country.

Us Mexicans have been in all the wars. I fought in all the wars of people who looked like me: Kuwait, Grenada, Iraq, Panama, Haiti.

I saw a lot of wounded Latinos during the riots in South Central, mostly hernias from lifting refrigerators and running too fast. You might have seen me on 911. I was the one who said, "Lift with your legs, not with your back."

In Grenada, I got shot. I fought in Panama, killed Panamanians. They looked like me. In South Central, it wasn't so bad. Pico Union was tough. I was defending a Payless. Well, those guys outside the store wanted to pay a lot less. I had to defend a shoe store.

So, after the riots in South Central, I wanted out. I should have left after the parade and the appearance with Tony Orlando singing "Tie a Yellow Ribbon Round the Old Oak Tree" during "Desert Storm." That was a good war.

When I left the military, I decided to use my training and landed a good job as a manager at a McDonalds. The battlefield ain't nothing compared to fifteen cars backed up during lunch hour: Some seventeen-year-old manager yelling at you because your fry cook is wounded while the screams of wounded minimum-wage workers fills the air. It was hell!

Now I work on the border patrol. It's peaceful here. Yeah, I'm out here watching point for America. Now I'm fighting an invasion, and there's not been a shot fired.

My favorite thing is to stop a suspicious car and knock on the trunk and say, "José, come out. We're here!" Nine out of ten of the guys are named José. Everyone wants to come to America!

Immigration, it started with the Indians crossing the Bering Strait to come here. The Mexicans crossing the Río Grande and the Pilgrims crossing the Atlantic.

I found a guy on the other side of the road, a Mexican. He was dead. Lying there in some boots and jeans. He looked like a cowboy. He looked like me. He looked just like me. I stared at his face and swore I was looking at a mirror.

But I'm an American and he's a Mexican. Now, why did he try to cross the highway? We put up signs... *(In bad Spanish.)* "Por amore de Dios no crizzen deo auto pizza!" They know it's illegal. But here he was, dead, staring up at the stars. He wanted to get to America, immigrate just like everyone else, to come here. 'Cause this land is Eden for the rest of the world.

I looked down at him and I remembered this story. See, Adam and Eve had all these children. One day, all the sons and daughters decided to explore creation. They went off in four different directions and promised to meet one day to share what they had discovered. After many generations had passed, the sons and daughters met in a dark forest. As they approached each other, they could hear but not see the other tribe coming. They got scared, so they beat their spears against their shields, which only scared each other more. *(Rhythmically.)* They beat their spears against their shields. They beat their spears against their shields...

Finally, they grew closer to one another till they filled the sky with arrows and spears and there was a terrible slaughter before they all discovered they were brothers and sisters...

I must have read that in *Soldier of Fortune* magazine. That dead Mexican could have been my brother. We looked so much alike. I remember thinking that maybe he was my brother, maybe this illegal alien was my brother. Maybe we're all brothers and sisters separated by a few generations. I looked at him and something woke up in me. I was enlightened. I made a vow. I decided I ain't hassling people who look like me. It ain't right. It all has got to stop. I don't want to fight or arrest people who look like him. But I've got to follow orders.

So every time you liberals pass the San Clemente border checkpoint, you can just stop flipping me off under your dashboards, 'cause I'm doing my job to stop the aliens. *(Gets angry.)* Yeah, I'm going to pull over everyone who looks like an alien, but they'll just be any blue-eyed, light-skinned aliens, blonde-haired Aryans. They could be illegal British or illegal Norwegian aliens or illegal Canadian aliens taking hockey jobs from Americans. You can never tell. You've got to be on your guard. Yeah, I am getting the aliens.

Hey, you in the Saab, pull it over, Sven. Let's see your papers. You don't have any? I knew it! Green card? You don't have one? I knew it. Get out of your car. All right! I got another illegal alien.

If the original Mexican border patrol had pulled over more Anglos, this would have still been Mexico. *(He starts to walk off stage.)*

Hey, Siegfried and Roy in the Mercedes, pull it over. Hey, Dudley and Mick in the Bentley, pull it over. Let's stop these aliens. I'm going to stop all those goddamn aliens. Bubba, pull over, turn down your country music!

9. FIDEL

The Mexican national anthem plays. Then in the darkness, a picture flashes of the San Onofre border checkpoint. We see a sign that says "Watch for pedestrians." A man walks on stage dressed in cowboy boots, Calvin Klein jeans, a big belly and a cowboy hat. Rick is now Fidel, a new macho. He carries a large suitcase and holds a tropical drink. He screams a grito. This is his last time crossing the border.

FIDEL: Ayyyyyyyyyy, Ay, I caught myself in my zipper. I was at the airport trying to buy a cheap ticket to Puerto Vallarta for a vacation. I deserved one. The pressure of being head busboy at Spago's is incredible. All of a sudden, there are these I.N.S. guys checking the papers of anyone who looks like a minority. They don't even see me. They're hassling some poor Mexican American guy on a "Love Connection" date to San Antonio to visit the *Alamo.* He's really unlucky, a guaranteed non-score weekend. So, I think, what's the worst they can do to me? Deport me back to Puerto Vallarta for free?

Well, I run up to them and say, "Please, don't send me back to that hellhole, Puerto Vallarta! I could not stand laying on the beach with cocoa butter in my face. I could not take another shrimp taco. Please don't deport

me to Puerto Vallarta or Ixtapa or Cancun." Before I
know it, I am being deported to Puerto Vallarta. The bastards put me on a Club Med flight to Vallarta. I earned
one thousand frequent deportation miles.

I am with American women in Brazilian string biki-
nis and yuppie guys drinking margaritas. I had waited on
half these guys at Spago's.

In Vallarta, life is good. I can buy fish barbecued on
the beach and drink tequila from coconuts. I walk on the
beach with my wife. I breathe my own air. I walk on my
own land holding my head up high, 'cause pride don't cost
you nothin'. 'Cause all us machos got is our pride, our
balls, our hearts and our strong hands.

I wear a *vaquero* outfit. I get a hat and boots and
jeans and I dress like a cowboy. I dress like a *vaquero*
because the first cowboys were Mexican, even though now
all you ride range over is a few tables at Spago's bringing
water. I look great and I am in Mexico.

Then all of a sudden, money runs out. I can't even eat
in the restaurants that Americans eat at. So I look to
America. She lures me. She seduces me. She's like those
women at the dance halls. From far away they look good,
but up close *"Ay, más Maybeline, por favor."*

I watch television and I see Doris Day speaking in
English. Before I know it, I'm in front of this *pinche* sign.
*(A warning sign of a man running across the freeway, like
a deer-crossing sign.)* This sign here shows you where to
cross. No one can figure out Anglos.

I got a gift for my Anglo girlfriend, the waitress. She
loves me. It's a piece of the pyramid. I told her a thousand
years ago, we mapped the stars and built great pyramids
and were the sons of a powerful civilization. She said,
"Well, Fidel, what have you done lately?" Well, I'm about
to run the fifty-yard dash. I plan to break my record.
*(Olympic theme music plays. The voice of an announcer
speaks.)*

V.O.: Welcome to the Third World Olympics. Fidel's been carbo loading for this event, getting ready to run. When he's not competing, he's a busboy. Although the Cubans excel in the rowing event, the Mexicans have always excelled in this running event. Wow, there he goes! *(Fidel moves in slow motion as car headlights flash on a screen behind him.)*

V.O.: His main competition is a Buick with Texas license plates. I hear a car screech. It's a hit! A hit! *(The screen headlights strike Fidel. He puts his hands up to shield himself. He is caught in the car lights. In slow motion, he spins off stage. He's hit.)*

FIDEL: Oh, God, I'm hit. Shit, oh, that hurts. They didn't stop. They didn't stop. Can't they read the signs? Where's the border patrol when you need them? He didn't slow down. He didn't slow down.

Oh, this hurts. Shit. I ripped my Calvins. Oh, God, I'm hurt. I've got to get to work on Monday. I'm going to get fired. My Anglo girlfriend is going to get mad. If I'm not there, she'll assume I am with another woman 'cause I am a macho. Oh, God, this hurts.

(He rolls over.)

That's better. Look at the stars. There's so many. How could we count them all? I can't walk. Maybe I can fly. Oh, the pain. Oh the pain, a macho feels no pain... A macho feels no pain... A macho feels no pain...

FADE TO:

1O. EULOGY

Lights slowly dim. The dark stage hears the muffled sounds of a man weeping. Then a match is lit. Alejandro is in his room alone, wearing his tuxedo. He walks to the altar. He lights a candle in the middle of the Day of the Dead altar. He places a flower on the altar. He looks at the audience and says the following quietly and simply:

ALEJANDRO: I lost my compadre today. I lost my friend. That's the way life is. I'll drink to him on The Day of the Dead. That's why life is sweet. It's fragile, it's illusionary, contrary.

Today, I lost a friend. I went to his funeral!

They put him in a box. He was meant to live free. He was killed, crossing a highway.

A macho should be killed by a bull. He should be shot by a rival lover, not gored to death by a wild Pontiac. That's no way to die.

I guess nothing lasts forever, especially us. Our flesh is sweet, but it is weak. It is fragile. It disappoints our macho spirits. I have lost you, my friend. Years ago, I lost my grandfather, my mother and father. They slipped from my warm hands into death's stronger hands. *(He lights candles.)*

Everything decays, ends, finishes. Nothing lasts. I lost my friend today. But today, I'll bring him his favorite beer and place it on the altar to remember him. This is for you, Fidel, your favorite. *(He takes a drink.)* He won't mind. It's a twelve-pack. Here's his favorite burrito. This is for you, Fidel. *(He eats it.)* Damn, that's good! It was just a bite. *(He picks up Fidel's wallet.)* Here's a picture of his girlfriend. She's good looking—I must comfort her. *(He pulls out some bills from his wallet.)* Fidel, I'll always remember that you owed me fifty dollars. *(He takes the money from the wallet.)* But today... *(Pause.)* Today... I feel too much. Today I, uh, I, oh, the pain! I'm a macho. A macho has a big heart. I feel big pain. We can love and feel so much, too much!

I will never forget your memory, Fidel. I will always remember you, except when I think of her. *(He points to a beautiful woman in audience.)*

Wow, you are pretty. You are so... *(He stops, holds his stomach in pain.)*

Oh, the pain! I know what you're thinking. I see it in your eyes. You think I'm just a busboy. Well, I'm not just a busboy. I'm a macho and I can take pain. I can feel the pain of the macho. Do you think I know no pain or feeling? Us machos feel more than any male. Do you think it is easy to be like me? Do you not know how I envy others who live with half the senses I do? Half the emotions? Half the hunger? Half the yearning? Half the life with half the fire in their loins with half the loins I got?

I am controlled by the moons. I'm a victim of the planets, a slave of the stars. I must love life! I must love women! I am ruled by their looks, their smells, the triangle between the nape of their neck and their ears and the other triangles on their mysterious bodies. Mysteries, I must have answers for.

Answers that drive me on like Ponce De León in the swamps of Florida, like Columbus in the New World, seeking answers for questions that only a macho could dare ask. Forced on and on when I only wish to rest... there is no rest... driven and whipped on by the pain of the macho. The pain of knowing I will never witness the birth of my children or never hold a conversation where I use expressions like "I hear what you're saying," or "I validate your feelings." Never to use words like "mauve" or "ditto." The pain of never tasting salt tears on my face. To know men like me are few and far between. When we meet, we must kill one another, *(Angrily.)* because a macho lives fully and damn the consequences. A macho knows more than anyone that he is mortal and that his flesh will decay. His giant spirit held in his weak frail body will one day be betrayed by old age. No lie will save us from death. We will die holding our hands uselessly against time, against being beaten down by the false hope of minimum wage, by the false hope of winning the Lotto, by the false hope of the American Dream—knowing our lives will be brief and of no consequence. *(He crumbles to the floor.)*

We will leave no pyramids this time, no great monuments, only a mountain of bills and the dust of our broken promises.

Busboy? I'm not just a busboy. I'm a macho. And as long as I believe I'm a macho, I want to be just a busboy. Hate me if you will, but only after you understand the pain of the macho. *(Beat.)* I lost my friend. Would you take me home and hold me? Thank you; you are so beautiful. *Ay*, she's beautiful!

Music and lighting now match the first scene and so does the dialogue. As Alejandro walks off stage, we hear:

I used to date this Anglo woman; she was beautiful like you, and we fell in love. I guess dating is stretching it a bit, but it was a very intense couple of hours.

FADE OUT.

A Corrido is heard as the lights fade down.

GLOSSARY OF MACHO TERMS

BY: DR. STEVE SANCHEZ, Ph.D., CHICANO STUDIES PROFESSOR

1. ***Anglo*:** A minority group living in the Southwest in the next ten years.
2. ***Anita Hill:*** No friend of Judge Thomas. See Judge Mandingo.
3. ***Ay:*** exclamation; Wow.
4. ***Babalú:*** Cuban word. Expression meaning give me your red head; also, name of an African God.
5. ***Barrio:*** Neighborhood, like where Mr. Rogers lives, or homeboy habitat.
6. ***Cabrones:*** Anglo term of endearment. (At least, that's what Latinos tell them.)
7. ***Calvins:*** Designer jeans; Chicano formal wear.
8. ***Cholo(a):*** Homeboy or girl; see homey.
9. ***Chuy:*** Name of my best friend.
10. ***Columbus:*** Rude Italian tourist.
11. ***Con Safos, ese:*** With protection.
12. ***Coño:*** Wow, Damn, Fuck, Man; common expression after slamming car door on fingers.
13. ***Corrido:*** Mexican song.

14. ***Day of the Dead:*** Day on which Mexicans remember the dead.
15. ***Desert Storm:*** Political public-relations trick.
16. ***Dudley and Mick:*** Dudley Moore and Mick Jagger, aging British stars.
17. ***Estrella:*** Star; what Erik Estrada used to be;* large flaming ball of gas, see Rush Limbaugh. (*Since this book's publication, I have directed Erik and feel I cannot say this anymore but could not drop this line from the original manuscript. Have I gone Hollywood?)
18. ***Evita:*** Rude Argentine. Gold mine for British composer Andrew Lloyd Webber.
19. ***Feministas:*** Group of macho-hating women.
20. ***Folklórico:*** Folk Dance ritual performed before every Chicano event; also used as a sleeping aid.
21. ***Gabachos:*** White people; set up for ethnic jokes.
22. ***Gloria Steinem:*** Feminista.
23. ***Grito:*** Scream, yell. Can be caused by squeezing your *huevos rancheros.*
24. ***Hillary Clinton:*** Anglo Evita.
25. ***Homey:*** Homeboy, neighborhood friend, bon vivant.
26. ***INS:*** Immigration and Naturalization Service. People in Beverly Hills calmly call it the day before they pay their help.
27. ***Iron Juan:*** Male issue book by Dr. Steve Sánchez, currently on sale.
28. ***ITT TECH:*** trade school.
29. ***Junta:*** Together, political term for group of Latinos getting together for a cause, very rare.
30. ***Judge Mandingo:*** See Judge Thomas.
31. ***Ladrones:*** Thieves.
32. ***Last of the Mexhicans:*** An Anglo fantasy novel where only one Mexican is left in the U.S.
33. ***Lotto:*** Mexican trust fund.
34. ***Love Connection:*** Television dating game.

35. *Low Rider Magazine:* Automobile engine weekly periodical.
36. *Macho:* A good masculine man; or a bad, chauvinistic man.
37. *Machacas:* Female machos; from the verb machacar, to shred the beef.
38. *Mad Doggin':* Giving a threatening gesture, i.e. President Kennedy was mad doggin' Castro.
39. *Mata:* To kill; from the verb *matar.*
40. *Madonna:* She's like a virgin, but not.
41. *Manteca Lard:* Reason for Jenny Craig.
42. *Martina Navratilova:* Tennis player; see *machaca.*
43. *Maybeline:* Purple eye shadow brand sold in gallon containers in the barrio.
44. *Mierda:* Feces; fertilizer left on lawns by pit bulls.
45. *Órale:* All right, cool, bitchin', also form of sex people have, i.e. She gives good *órale.*
46. *Panza:* Stomach.
47. *Pinche:* Fucking (adj.)
48. *Pedo:* Flatulence; a faux pas in the Space Shuttle.
49. *Placa:* Name or "tag" spray painted on a wall.
50. *Ponce De León:* Rude Spanish tourist.
51. *Phil Donahue:* Male *feminista.*
52. *Quinceañeras:* Ritual of fifteen-year-old Mexican debutantes; cause of major bankruptcy in the barrio.
53. *Red Onion:* Restaurant known for its great meat market.
54. *Riot:* Civil insurrection in Los Angeles. I was there; it was a riot.
55. *Rush Limbaugh:* See *mierda.*
56. *Sabes Qué:* Sp. for You know what?
57. *Salsa:* #1. Condiment in the U.S.; 2. fast dance in the U.S. invented by Puerto Ricans and danced badly by Mexicans.
58. *Siegfried & Roy:* A magic couple.
59. *Spago's:* Trendy restaurant in L.A. run by Wolfgang Puck.
60. *Standard Brand Paints Store:* Undocumented workers social club.

61. ***Sweet-N-Low:*** Artificial sweetener.
62. ***T & A:*** Tits and ass.
63. ***Vaquero:*** Mexican cowboy.
64. ***Vato:*** Guy, dude, man, potential gardener.
65. ***Viva:*** Hooray, life; also special brand of toilet paper.
66. ***911***: The number Chicanos call when they want to be put on hold; also TV show.

LATINOLOGUES

MONOLOGUES OF THE LATIN EXPERIENCE

What the critics say...

"Najera's monologues burst from the barrio to the universal."
                                              —L.A. Weekly

"Najera's monologues peer deeply into the uncertainties of culture."
                                    —Los Angeles Times

"No one escapes Najera's biting satire."   **—La Opiníon**

Additional monologues can be taken out from Pain of the Macho and replaced in Latinologues or vice versa. The reason I chose the monologue form is to illustrate that the search for identity is an individual undertaking, not a group cultural journey. The monologue form also allows the performers to create a one-on-one relationship between performer and audience which is the experience we hope to achieve in a day-to-day interaction.

Each character will be introduced with a prerecorded piece of music. The sets will be minimal. The costumes and the music will suggest the characters and mood of the scenes.

P.S. These characters all come from real persons I have met. R.N.

Credits:

Writer:
   Rick Najera
Director:
   Rick Najera
Producer:
   Charo Toledo.
Associate Producer, Publicist:
   Paul Saucido
Logo/ Map of the World/ Banner Designer:
   José Ramírez
Scroll Designer:
   Sergio Zenteno
Light Designer:
   Yuki Uehara
Sound Designer:
   Mark Torres
Stage Manager:
   Lalo Medina
Catering Opening Night Party:
   Rachel from Little Ricky's Restaurant

Ensemble: **Gilbert Esquivel, Gil Ferrales, Katherine Franco Steeves, John Furse, Luchy Garcia, Dante Garza, Jennifer Lamar, Luis Raúl, Martin Morales, Rudy Moreno, Chi Chi Navarro, Rick Najera, Emilio Rivera, Rodney Rincón, Charro Toledo, Monica Torres.**

LATINOLOGUES

The show can be performed by a group of actors or by male and female actors.

Order of the Show:

Mexican Moses: **Rick Najera**
Manic Hispanic: **Gil Ferrales**
Slow Guy: **Gilbert Esquivel**
Typical Latina Mother: **Chi Chi Navarro**
Josephine: **Charo Toledo**
Fat Matador: **Luis Raúl**
Cuba Libre: **Monica Torres**
Art: **John Furse**
Bufford Gomez: **Rudy Moreno**
Mexican Moses: **Rick Najera**

Notes from Rick:

If you came to see "The Pain of my People," you will be disappointed. Latinologues is a celebration of flawed and won-derful people that strive for moments of poetry in a life filled with the ridiculous. There is not one Latino experience in these monologues; there are many. The only thing these characters truly share is a need to be heard and understood. We as a people are not easily defined, so neither are our writings. We vary from the superficial to the profound, from the tragic to triumphant; each with our own Latino point of view.

I chose to have characters speak in a monologue because that is the feeling among Latinos today. We are shipwrecked and alone in defining ourselves in a changing world; unable to dialogue, to be heard. We warm ourselves by the "Cool fire" of television and do not see ourselves represented in the United States. If we do, it's in a stereotypical fashion. So, I write with my voice, my reality. All I can do is write what I hear, not what others would have me say.

The evening is a collection of monolouges on the Latino experience. These characters are all different and unique, but they all crave to be understood. That is a human need, not just a Latino need. I needed to tell these tales. If I don't tell the story you wish to hear tonight, please be assured I plan to tell your Latino tale soon. After all, there are millions of Latinologues out there. This is just a beginning.

1. MEXICAN MOSES TAKES ON THE WORLD

Lights go to half as the pre-show music ends. We go from a beautiful corrido to the theme from Cecil B. De Mille's The Ten Commandments. *A white person's voice introduces Mexican Moses. Mexican Moses appears on stage. He holds a large staff in his hand. He says nothing, but looks biblical and serious. The music fades as the stage goes dark. On a darkened silent stage, behind Mexican Moses, there is a large map of the world that is revealed on the back stage wall. It resembles an old Spanish-style map of the world, labeled fourteen ninety-two. It is one of the old yellowed maps of the Americas. He holds a bullhorn in his hand. He is dressed in a serape and yammuca with dingo balls. He has a neo-biblical Chicano look. He steps forward and lifts his staff. He is carrying a black-looking paper-maché tablet that holds the four Cinco de Mayo commandments. A voice over is heard over the Cecil B. De Mille's* The Ten Commandments *music.*

ANNOUNCER: It came about in the time of the cruel pharaoh Pete Wilson. A child was found floating down the East L.A. River in a Raiders' ice chest. He was clad in peneltons and khaki swaddling clothes. He was found by a daughter of a Republican and was raised, not as a Mexican, but as an Anglo. He did not know he was Latino except for a high tolerance for lawn blowers and a fascination with *banda* music. He was called Mexican Moses.

MEXICAN MOSES: Pete Wilson, let my people go free. Pete Wilson, let my people go free. I am he, Mexican Moses. I was found floating down the East L.A. River in a Raiders' ice chest. I was clad in peneltons and khaki swaddling clothes. I was found by a daughter of a Republican and was raised, not as a Mexican, but as an Anglo. I am Mexican Moses.

Once it was discovered that I was Mexican, I was banished to the deserts of Bakersfield. The desert, where harsh winds blow and cold nights mold prophets. I spent many cold nights alone. Yet I did not touch myself. *(Looks to the audience of disbelievers.)* I didn't, for I was on a holy mission. I almost died in the desert, but miraculously I found an overturned catering truck burning, and found food and drink. I found and drank a bottle of *horchata* light, half the calories and all the taste. I had a tamale and an egg-salad sandwich. I was refreshed until the mayonnaise hit my system, for it had been in the sun. Next, I tried to get help at Bakersfield General Hospital. But because of Proposition 187, I lost my room to an illegal Swede. It was then that I heard a small, still voice. *(A stern Edward James Olmos-type voice is heard).*

MEXICAN GOD VOICE: "Mexican Moses, I'm talking to you *vato*. I have heard the *gritos* of my people and I have seen the passing of Proposition 187, and it does not please me. I send earthquakes, riots, floods and fire to California. What more do these people want, Godzilla walking down Hollywood Boulevard, before they realize I'm not happy? Mexican Moses, lead my people, for I have heard their *gritos* and I know their trouble, for you are Mexican Moses." (Kneels humbly.)

And I said, "I don't look anything like Charleston Heston." And God said, "Neither did the first Jewish Moses."

And God said to go to the swap meet where I shall find all the Latinos. And here you are. Latinos, this will be known as our Exodus: Latino Exodus prop one eighty-seven. This will be one of our most holy nights, and I'm not talking about the Big Spin. It is on this night we remember a great event other than a Julio César Chávez fight. I'm talking about Latino Exodus. All at this swap meet, hear my voice.

Hey, you with the six-pack of tube socks, listen up.

Latinos, follow me! We will wander in the desert, and we won't even need a Thomas Guide. I'll lead us. Tortillas from heaven will feed us, and there will be... *(Sirens are heard.)*

Hey, you with the *carne asada*, get away from my burning bush. I need that. We will learn many commandments such as:

"Thou shall not use the name of Edward James Olmos in vain." Or: "Thou shall pay for your cable television installation." And: "Thou shall love thyself as the Cubans love themselves." Most importantly: "Thou shall be on time."

Now, the tribe of Cuba to the far right, Chicanos to the far left, Mexican Americans to the moderate middle. We leave tonight. All the illegal aliens, Republican maids, form a separate line. Wow, so many! Puerto Ricans, we leave tonight. Only two chickens per family: one for eating, one for sacrifice. No, I don't want to hear from you Dominicans—the Puerto Ricans didn't even want me to invite you. Central Americans, I am not with immigration; you can trust me.

Where's the Brazilians? Well, they shall be known as the lost tribe. The president of Peru, Mr. Fugimoro, you cannot come with us. Xuxa, put on some clothes; this is a holy journey. Get in line. By the way, Xuxa, you will not be in charge of child care. I'd like some non-Aryan role model for our kids.

Argentineans, you must get in line. Get in line! Argentineans, you are not Europeans, you are Latinos. I repeat, you are *not* European.

Okay, Chicanos, Hispanics, Latinos, Mexican Americans. Let's agree on just one thing for once. Let's put aside our petty differences and just try to agree for once. Let's start with something simple. What shall we be called? Hispanic? Latino? Chicano? Latin American? Americans of Latino descent? How about children of the sun? That's kind of flashy. Let's agree on a name we would like to be called before we go. *(Riot is heard.)*

Oh, Lord, these hardheaded Latinos. Why can't we agree? Get back in line. I'm Mexican Moses. *(Mexican Moses starts to leave.)*

Don't give that Cuban an espresso. He'll kill himself. Get this Guatemalan off my leg!

ANNOUNCER: And so started the greatest Latin Exodus seen since the end of *La Bamba.*

BLACK OUT.

2. MANIC HISPANIC

"Sabotage," by the Beastie Boys, plays. It's hard and driving. He or she is an expensively dressed, light-skinned Latino/Latina. The Manic Hispanic is in his/her postmodern office. We see an expensive large desk and a big leather executive chair behind it. Manic Hispanic sits on his/her chair as the lights come up. The performer's back is to the audience.

MANIC HISPANIC: Nice view, great view, huh? You're wondering why God smiled on me. Maybe it's a quota system. Maybe I don't deserve it. "I'm the universe expressing itself. I deserve wealth and happiness. I deserve an espresso." *(Manic Hispanic turns around.)*

Phil, bring me an espresso. Never hire Anglos—they won't work. I don't care about the prestige.

I have to remember that it's okay to love me.

I was so messed up before I went to therapy. I even tried psychics. I went to a psychic. She told me I had three past lives. I said, "Stop the karma merry-go-round, I want to get off."

She said that I was an Egyptian eunuch in the twelfth century. That explains my fascination with castration. Then she says I was a Chinese concubine in the thirteenth century. That explains my fascination with silk. Then in 1940, I was a Mexican taxi driver who was beaten to death at a piñata party by a deaf eight-year old. That explains my fascination with baseball, 'cause I'm not Dominican.

Wow, three past lives. Talk about bad luck: a minority in three past lives. God, why couldn't I be British royalty just once? Why do I get the boring past lives? Well, life's unfair. Some people are unlucky. But not me and not anymore. I got lucky. I got well and, now, it's my turn to make other Latinos lucky.

And right now, you got lucky. Life smiled on you because I loved your script: *Cortez and Montezuma*. What a great film! Cortez and Montezuma, what wonderful characters. I see Jeremy Irons and Paul Rodríguez in the leading roles. You did make Cortez look like a bad guy. But we can lighten him up in the rewrites, especially if we get Robin Williams to play Cortez, to bring out Cortez's comedic side... or Jim Carrey. We can emphasize Cortez's discovery of this great culture and downplay the massive destruction of it.

This market is going to be huge.

I even adopted a little Latino kid to start. I have this problem with commitment. My roommate Enrique/Erica said I should do something nice, so I adopted this little Third-World Latino kid. There's his picture on the wall. He's the one with the flies on his forehead. I'm just worried that someday I'll get a knock at my door. I'll see some kid saying, "You remember me? I got one stinking letter and a few pennies a day. I'm Paco from Peru." *(She/He laughs when she/he realizes there's no response.)*

It feels good to help out a fellow Hispanic. I'm Hispanic. That's why the studio felt I would have a perspective on this project. I know what you're thinking. Am I Latino enough to get your project? Have I experienced the pain of my people? *(Beat.)*

Uh... no. But I'm full Mexican. I don't care what that nasty rumor says. I'm pure Mexican. I'm just light. My sister's dark; she's got a lot of Indian blood. I know that, 'cause when I was young, I used to have her build me Spanish missions in my back yard and I converted her to Catholicism. I stole her gold jewelry and gave her chicken pox. *(Beat.)*

That was a joke. You Chicanos are very serious.

I went to a Chicano Studies Program. They thought that I wasn't Chicano. "Oh, please, let me join your oppressed minority group." They felt I hadn't felt enough oppression. And I said, "Pepe, does right now count?"

I can't speak a word of Spanish, but that doesn't make me less of a minority.

I was on a plane once and a stewardess came up to me and said, "Are you an Hispanic?" I said, "Yes, but I'm not leaving first class." I thought it was going to be one of those Rosa Parks-back-of-the-bus moments. So I said, "Yes." Then she said, "This man is having medical difficulties; we need you to translate using your best Spanish possible." So I walked up to the man and said, *(Heavy Spanish accent.)* "Chew are going to die." I speak horrible Spanish. But I'm still Hispanic. *(Calms down.)*

Do you like that? I got that statue at Cancun. Great Mayan pyramids in Cancun. I went to Cancun in a Club Med weekend to get in touch with my indigenous roots with my roommate. She/He has full lips, strong muscles and is a beautiful tennis player. So I walked to the top of this newly discovered Mayan pyramid. I saw the mist of the jungle rise up as my people would have seen it thousands of years ago. *(Truly in awe and touched sincerely and simply.)*

I felt for once I belonged to something other than myself. I was truly touched. The confusion I sometimes feel vanished. I knew who I was, where I was from, where I was going. I was in the middle of it all, where it all began, and I knew peace. *(Confessional.)*

I'm very light and tall. My family must have been from the northern area of the Yucatan, near the Alps. So, I'm on top of this Mayan pyramid and I see this little Indian head hidden in the rocks. I was touched. No one had seen this little sculpture for over a thousand years, and I was in awe.

My Mayan side was in awe, but my Spanish conquistador side thought it would've made a neat bookend. So I broke it off and brought it here and made it into an ashtray. *(The spell is gone and the Manic Hispanic is back.)*

You can put your cigarette butts right there, in the Indian's head. All right, we've bonded. *(Angrily with menace.)*

Now, about your script: let's make Cortez look like the good guy.

BLACK OUT.

3. THE ART OF BEING COMFORTABLE
WHILE YOU FEEL
UNCOMFORTABLE

A very earnest young man enters. He has tights on and dark clothing. On a screen behind him headlines read, "Mexican youth with spray can in his hand shot by Anglo." He looks like a performance-art-type wanna-be: blonde wig, cigarette dangling in his mouth. Sounds of a press conference are heard. Lights flash as if photographs are being taken. Lights reveal a man in mid performance, with a bad performance-art style.

ART: Thank you for attending this news conference. I know I have received a lot of attention after shooting the Mexican gang tagger recently. Some people have labeled me a vigilante, like Charles Bronson. Well, I say it's not true. I've seen all his movies a thousand times. I'm nothing like him. I'm no vigilante. I'm a performance artist. I do art.

I want to say this former Marine and part-time actor, this performance artist has turned tragedy to art. I have created a one-man show on this tragedy. I would like to give you just a little taste of the show from my new solo work. *(He goes into a bad performance art style.)* "Drop the Magic Marker before I kill you."

Hey, Mr. Tagger man! Why are you writing on that wall? Why are you making me feel scared and guilty?

You messed up these walls with your angry ignorance. But I'll write down your license-plate number. I'll write down your license-plate number, twice. Oh no! You got a screwdriver. *(To audience.)* Luckily, I was bringing my gun to be repaired.

(In character.) I'm Daniel Boone, in this urban Alamo, and you're a shaved-headed Indian.

Luckily, I've got ammunition on my long-barreled friend.

Speak to him, long-barreled friend, speak to him. *(He looks around.)*

Halt, I say, for I have written down your license plate. *(The gun goes off.)* Oh no, my gun went off!

We both are the victims in this urban drama. *(He reaches hands in the air.)*

Why, oh Lordy, why? *(Beat.)* White man's burdened blues. Thank You. I have received a lot of praise recently for shooting that gang tagger. I hate to see the loss of life or ammunition, but when I saw that Mexican with the can of spray paint in his hand, I knew what I had to do. I shot him and wounded his fellow gang member.

Well, I was acquitted, and I didn't have to serve a day in prison, which was a good thing. 'Cause, you know, I probably would have gotten gang-raped. I would have been walking around saying, "Menthol or filtered? Don't touch me! I'm T-Bone's girl!" Then I could at least perform at Highways and get some funding as a gay artist. *(Laughs.)* Oh, I kid! Lets get serious, enough fun.

As you could see tonight, I do cutting-edge white, heterosexual male, one-man drama. It seems no one wants to hire that anymore. This shooting helped in a way. I got lots of publicity. Well, after I shot the gang tagger, before he used his can of paint on me. I could have been killed like that girl in *Goldfinger*.

At first, I was seen as a hero, but I consider myself just an ordinary citizen and part-time performance artist. I want to set the record straight and say I had nothing to do with the recent shooting of the Chicano muralist. That was someone else. It was wrong: not every Mexican painting on a wall is a criminal... *(Suspiciously.)*... if that's what he really was doing.

I have toured my one-man show, my "Family Alamo," for years to enthusiastic responses. But of course, with this climate of liberal political anti-American sentiment going around, it was very difficult for me to perform. No one wants to hear what a white heterosexual man is thinking. We don't matter. Well, it hurts. I'm an artist, and sometimes we must feel hurt or hurt others for inspiration. Talking about inspiration, let me show you a scene from my "Family Alamo." *(He gets into a bad acting stance, totally unaware of his bad acting style.)*

"Well, Danny Boone, those murdering heathen Mexicans are sneaking up on us. Trying to take the Alamo. Look how they slink up to the wall using white women to shield them!"

Well, at that moment, I got booed. It was worse than singing "Ebony and Ivory," at Amateur Night at the Apollo. I sang the first verse, then all I remember was this bright light and then hearing my grandma's voice, and then an excruciating pain and a liquid diet for a month.

Where was I? I didn't shoot that Mexican tagger for no reason. I'm not a vigilante. I'm an artist. I love minorities. I have played minorities. I'm an actor. I can play any of them.

I did the Manzanar drama seen through the eyes of a Japanese man interred in Manzanar. But did the Japanese appreciate me? No. You can't please these minorities. Would you mind if I did a little of my NRA award-winning show for you all? Now a scene from my *Little Manzanar: (In a bad Japanese accent.)*

"Oh, it is good I'm here instead of outside these barbed wires. I might be tempted to sabotage the American war effort. I have learned so many things here, and the desert air has cured my asthma. Sergeant Roy, you know, your radio could be made smaller. Gee, what beautiful sunsets we have here in wonderful Manzanar." *(Art waits for applause.)*

Thank you. *(He bows. He gives that exhausted-performer-having-given his-all bow.)*

I did a one man show about Martin Luther King. Not because he is just a Black hero, he's a human hero.

Unfortunately, the King estate would not give me permission to do any of his speeches or writings. So I was forced to take imagined moments of his life. It goes something like this:

(He does a thick, bad Southern black man accent.)

"Coreta, boy, I better get to sleep. I have that big speech ahead of me tomorrow. Uh, you know, let's forget the speech or any other of my writings. Let's concentrate on other things. *(Beat.)*

"Boy, is it hot today! Do you want some lemons and ade? Do I smell barbecue or is the clan in town? Coreta, bring me a paper! I'm going to be here awhile." *(Bows.)*

Thank you.

I think one-man shows are the art of feeling comfortable while being uncomfortable. I have gotten a lot of criticism for my work, but I think it's because I show beloved figures from history in a sometimes unflattering light. Like when I played Harvey Milk in "Boy, can I get on my co-worker's nerves," or, "I need a twinkie." People in Frisco booed me. So, about shooting the tagger... he was destroying property, so I did what anyone who was just as well-armed would have done. But I say forgive and forget. I even gave his family tickets to my last show, group rate. Any questions? *(Someone tries to ask him a question, but he cuts them off. Or if they do ask a question, he does not answers it.)*

I'm single.

Oh, I'm happy to report I'm on my fifth call-back for Montezuma in *Montezuma and Cortez*, the movie. My great-grandmother was part Cherokee, so don't you write any letters. I plan to buy a tanning booth. Any other questions? *(Sincerely.)* Uh, before I go, remember to support your local artist. And remember, us artists sometimes must take from our own personal tragedy, or if we have no personal tragedy we sometimes have to create them. But more importantly, if you are in a bad neighborhood and you decide to fight crime, remember you may not be a trained actor, so leave crime fighting to professionals like us.

FADE OUT.

4. THE LAST OF THE MEXIHICANS

A Chicano with a brown beret hat walks on stage. He has a Che Guevera T-shirt on and a "No Grapes" button on. He is a very passionate, dark-skinned Latino. He stands with a megaphone.

THE LAST OF THE MEXIHICANS: Would you like some coffee, some grapes, huh? I bet you would, you little yuppie. Well, we don't serve that at this Chicano organization. We are down for brown. We don't eat grapes. We boycott them. We even boycott most desserts to show solidarity with diabetics. If you're not down, you can join a folklórico group. Let's begin your interview.

I don't know who you are, but I know who I am. I'm not confused. I'm angry, but not confused. I was created by the rape of our indigenous mothers by our Spanish forefathers. Death to Julio Iglesias. This interview will be done in English. We will use the hated language of our oppressor because, uh, unfortunately, I don't speak good Spanish.

I refuse to learn Spanish because it is the language of those paella-eating, lisping, conquering bastards who caused all the problems of the world. That is, until the white men came. They caused even more problems, followed by the hated Cuban oppressor, the Puerto Rican carpet bagger and the Mexican nationalist, who exploited the conquered Chicanos to take better jobs from us in Spanish-language commercials.

I should be speaking Nahual, but unfortunately our school system has denied us the chance to learn our mother language.

Because of my unfortunate formal last name, my slave name of Martínez, people assume I speak Spanish, which is a drag. I keep having this recurring nightmare with me, Fidel Castro and Kennedy during the Cuban

Missile Crisis. Kennedy wants me to translate in Spanish the peace message, and I can't. I don't know what the missiles symbolize.

I have no hated Spanish blood in me. I'm nearly pure Indio. I know I don't have real Indian features, but I'm working on it. I'm going to a plastic surgeon to see if I can get a more indigenous look. I'm going to get an Aztec nose job.

Now, some questions. Do you speak any other languages? *(Beat.)*

Wow, three. Uh, that's cool.

Uh, are you now or have you ever watched Rush Limbaugh?

Okay. Do you recognize and celebrate certain religious holidays that are important to our people, such as the birthday of Carlos Santana? Do you refuse to recognize the birth of Linda Ronstadt? Good. Have you ever listened to Howard Stern or were you ever a member of any Cuban or Republican groups? Do you want to be successful?

You do? Oh, man, you admitted it. I got you now. You admitted it. Oh, not too successful, and if you are, it's from the betterment of La Raza. Good. La Raza may call on you to drive me to school once in a while and lend me some *feria* for my *lonche*.

Do you know what a *cuchifrito* is, or *mofongo?* I'm going to say that word again: *mofongo.* Okay, you don't know what that is. I was testing you to see if you were an undercover Cuban or Puerto Rican. Those *mofongo*-eating fast-dancing non-consonant-pronouncing bastards are taking over.

They are invading our sacred land. We have been here for five hundred years. Then they show up and buy TV stations, speak Spanish really fast and they stick together.

Well, I say they cannot be allowed to join us Chicanos. We forbid any light-skinned Spanish, any Republicans or moderate Democrats, anyone that has had a grape in the last ten years or anyone who has complained about how I run this club.

Uh, I think that is the main reason there are only two Chicanos on this campus.

This Machaca Club Movimiento Aztlán Chicano Association Club of America is going through scandals. Especially since someone has taken our money for our dance: "Chicano Nights Remembering our Struggle, Pain, Suffering and Hardship." The celebration was not attended well and we lost our money.

I know there were some money questions, such as the question why our club stereo was residing in my dorm room. But we must be united around me, if we are to survive.

I like you. I think I'm going to let you join us. I have just finished fasting for over six hours, so I'm a little light-headed. I got a blood-sugar problem. You want to take me to lunch? Good.

We have to make sure that we keep this association Chicano exclusive. No Caribbeans or Cubans, please. The Cubans already have a promised land. It's called Miami. We don't have nothing. When a great leader like me must still live with his parents, something's wrong. We must stick together and rid our land of all non-Chicanos.

Can I get a *grito*? Someone give me a *grito*.

(He screams a grito.)

Oh, yes, if you know any Anglos who want to learn to *grito*, I will be giving a *grito* crash course after school. I will crash a hammer on their hand and they will *grito* and experience the pain of my people.

(He gets very animated.)

I dream of a day when we will be pure Chicano. When we will relive our glory days of the Aztlán, and live free and proud. I dream of a glory day when great leaders like myself will lead our people.

(Beat.)

Until then, we're going to be having a car wash this weekend to raise money for my tuition. Uh, you got any soap? You want to be on the soap committee? Congratulations. I'm going to let you join my oppressed minority club. Can I borrow $40 bucks from you? Initiation fee.

FADE OUT.

5. STOP AND LISTEN

A young Puerto Rican girl walks on stage holding her stomach. She listens with a stethoscope to her stomach. She is in a hospital gown. She wears no shoes, just slippers. She has an almost dazed, confused look about her. She puts the stethoscope to her belly and listens. Then she smiles. She looks directly at the audience and speaks with her New York accent.

RITA: Oh, my God, do you hear that? That's the most beautiful sound in the world. That's life.

This is a magic stethoscope. I can hear things. When I listen to my belly, I hear life, purring, murmuring, agitating, confounding, surprising, unending life. You gotta listen. Listening is important. People don't listen nowadays. That's how they learn to be indifferent.

They listen to only what they want to hear. I can say thousands of words, but, swear to God, guys only hear yes. You say yes to a guy. Believe me. He'll stop and listen. You say no, he won't hear you. He won't be listening. They don't ever hear no. Listening is important. But with a stethoscope you can hear everything.

Oh, I can hear her. I can still hear her. That's the sound of life. You got to listen to that sound of life. I made that. That's my baby. That's Barbie, who ain't never going to leave, like when I was a girl. One day, I was playing house in our apartment and I put my Cabbage Patch baby doll right next to me. *(She mimes putting doll down and rocking her.)* "Sit there, baby, while mom makes us some tea and mofongo."

I put my baby right down in front of me. Then I turned around and, when I did, my Cabbage Patch baby was ripped off.

My mother called it a little community garden-patch doll, because it wasn't real. Real Cabbage Patch dolls got adoption papers. Mine was an illegitimate Korean grocery store rip-off.

Well, okay, I lost my Cabbage Patch doll 'cause there was this Dominican girl. Oh, my God, I'll never forget her name, Connie. Connie, trying to sound all white. Her real name was Conchita Rosario Taviña Pumarejo. And she was so dark her parents would paint a white strip on her and send her out on Halloween as a Goodrich tire.

I'm not lying, swear to God. And she had real curly hair, kinky. If you're Puerto Rican and you got curly hair, people start asking to see your grandmother. *Y tu abuela ¿dónde esta?* If you hide your grandmother, it means you have a lot of black blood in you. Her grandmother was hidden back in her kitchen in Africa. She didn't want anyone to see her.

Well, she didn't like me 'cause my hair was permanent, not straightened.

(She puts stethoscope out to the audience.) I can hear what you're thinking—mine's a perm. So don't ask me about my *abuela*. No negritos in my family except for maybe my sister, who I know has got some African blood in her, 'cause I caught her practicing voodoo on my Cabbage Patch doll, with needles and stuff. She said she was sewing her dress up. I didn't believe her, you know. That's African behavior.

Back to my baby story: The bitch stole my Cabbage Patch kid, and by the time I got her back, it was a Cabbage Patch teenager.

But in my belly is my little doll that is never going to leave me. I made this life. I did. Now I got my own doll and no one can take my doll away. I made her here. She's made in the U.S.A., just like me.

And I'm getting all sorts of attention. All my friends are excited and people are talking about giving me their leftover baby clothes. And I know all about leftovers. I've had leftovers all my life.

My mother was a waitress. She used to bring me food home from a restaurant and I used to bug her by saying stuff like, "Hey, there's a cigarette butt in this steak." She'd get all mad and say, "It wasn't on anyone's plate. They're leftovers."

(She puts the stethoscope to her belly.) Can you hear it? That sound is life. My life, and it's loud, you know, like a subway drummer. I can put these things to the wall and hear lots of strange sounds. Like the way my Cuban neighbors talk real fast about how they're going to leave the Bronx some day and go back to where people speak their language, and where they won't be treated as foreigners, a place called Miami.

I got this stethoscope at the clinic. I use it now to listen real close for my baby. No one will take away my stethoscope. I need it. With a stethoscope you can hear things like the doctors talking about you, calling you another unwed Puerto Rican mother. Talking about how, "Just what the world needs: another unwed mother."

But I say fifty percent of marriages end in divorce, so I'm not an unwed mother. I'm a pre-divorced single mother—which ain't so bad.

I hear people talk about me all the time. But I don't care. I'm like the Virgin Mary with child, but my conception wasn't so divine or immaculate. Believe me. That car was uncomfortable and Junior was no God. He was dirty. He had just got off work. He looked good. He was in shape. I met him at my gym, an exclusive gym in Manhattan. Okay, I worked there, but it's still my gym. I cleaned it enough.

(To an audience member.)

Shut up. I heard you with my stethoscope. It gives me power. I can hear things. I stole this stethoscope from the doctor at the clinic. After the operation, I took it. I took it after they stole my baby. I wasn't consenting to nothing. I didn't want what they gave me.

(She starts to cry.)

I didn't want what they gave me. I didn't want to lose what they took from me. It was my baby, something that belonged to me. That baby could have had whatever she had wanted. She could have been anything she wanted to be. *(She curses in Spanish, pounds her fist on her sides and falls crying to the ground. Pause. Then she puts the stethoscope to her belly.)*

They weren't listening. They weren't listening to me. You got to listen.

(Listens with her stethoscope.) Yeah, I can still hear my baby. It's like an echo now. No, wait. I can hear life. I know it. They didn't take my baby away. That ain't no echo. There's still life in my belly. I know it with my stethoscope. I heard it. I just got to listen real hard. If I can listen hard, I'll hear life, but you got to listen. That's what life is. It's sound. It's heartbeat. And if you're deaf, you can feel sound beating in your belly. 'Cause life's got to get out. Life's got to move around. Listen. Can you hear my life? Can you hear my baby? I can still hear my baby. Can you hear me? Are you listening?

FADE OUT.

(Mexican Moses returns to stage as if he's walking through quickly. A spotlight hits him. He holds a map and clip board.)

MEXICAN MOSES: Turn off the car light—not the high beams. Anyone got a match or flashlight? Okay. Who's got the Thomas Guide? I can't take much of this grumbling.

The Lord has some more commandments for you:

"Thou shall get insured." Actually, it's just a suggestion. Whatever you think is right. If you feel lucky, don't get insurance.

If you win at Lotto, "Thou shall not say that you're going to keep your job and live as you always have." That really bothers out-of-work Anglos.

Fourth, "Thou shall return my big-screen TV." My big screen TV is missing. I know it was the *cholos* from the White Fence gang. Give it back to me!

Now, get back in line. Let's start moving. Oh, an announcement: The Rodríguez's need jumper cables. *(Mexican Moses walks off.)*

ANNOUNCER: And still, Mexican Moses traveled and more people joined the Exodus, and the numbers of the tribes swelled. After a Cinco de Mayo party and a corporate sponsorship by Dos Equis, the numbers really swelled, for they didn't believe in birth control and the beer was free.

BLACK OUT.

6. TOUGH LOVE

In the darkness, a match is struck, a candle is lit. Then lights reveal a woman walking onto the stage. She is wrapped in a Spanish mantilla. She sits down in her Lazy Boy chair and cracks open a beer.

TYPICAL LATINA MOTHER: *Ay*, Chata, sit down. So good to see you. Sorry about the lights, but they bother José. José, wake up. José, wake up! José is a good boy. He's so strong, so *macho*. I raised him well. I spoil him. All my boys are good boys, even Alfredo. His wife called me and told me he beat her, and I said to her, "What did you do?" He would never do that, 'cause he's a good boy.

You have to be loyal to your boys. Every marriage goes through trials and tribulations.

José, wake up. There's no light. I shuttered the windows and made you *menudo*. No, it's not a hangover. *Ay*, Chata, I worry about these kids! I don't know what to do nowadays.

I worry about my son. All the crime in the neighborhood, random violence, gangs. I miss El Salvador. In El Salvador, the death squads came to your house, took you away, you were dead. Professional. Here, the violence is random. I worry about José. I spoil him, but all Latina mothers spoil their children.

Like Dolores, who spoils her boy, the "professional bike rider." But of course, she has to spoil him; the poor boy is slow. And he's no professional bike rider, like she says! Huh! He has to wear that bike helmet because he's a... *(Loudly.)*... head-banger.

But you know, Chata, you have to love your boys and you have to be optimistic. Concentrate on the good. First, the good news. José's no longer gang-banging and spray-painting on walls or stealing the morning papers. It's a miracle. He has a direction in his life. So I owe the Virgin for answering my prayers. José, come down. There's no light. I covered the windows. No, Chata, it's not a hangover. It's worse. That's the bad news.

The bad news is he's a vampire. He's a vampire.

(Loudly.) A vampire! Yes, he's a vampire. *(The mother crosses herself.)*

He's one of the undead, a vampire. But at least he's not one of the undocumented. That would be worse. So I'm grateful about some things.

I don't mean to complain. I know. Every family has their problems. My José is a temporary vampire. It's just a phase. You don't know how hard it has been carrying this secret around.

I still remember the day I first saw the strange marks on his neck. I said, "Have you been seeing that *puta,* La Sad Girl?" He said, "No." Then he started buying ruffled shirts, black capes and hats. Then I noticed his hatred of crosses. You can imagine my embarrassment, we being Catholic and all. And me the head of the Daughters of the Inquisition committee. Then I started finding a few bodies drained of blood. That's when I said we should talk. That's when he told me, "Mamá, I'm a vampire." I said, "Thank God, I thought you were gay like María's boy, the one who danced with *Ballet Folklorico de Coco,* wanted a quinceañera, and tried to be queen of the Miss East L.A. Pageant."

Oh, my poor José, a vampire. You should hear him at night, wailing and screaming. At first, I thought it was the Puerto Ricans next door. I hear them at night "Oh, Papi; oh, Papi; oh, Mami." I was going to call *social services. Desgrasiados.* Sometimes doing the nasty, not for procreation, but for pleasure. *(She crosses herself.)*

I never did it for pleasure. It was two minutes of duty.

I just have to remain positive. A vampire isn't necessarily all that bad. At least, he's not like Lupita's boy, the "werewolf." Her son thinks he is a werewolf. That boy was bit by María's Chihuahua. So every full moon, he grows hair all over his body, pees on carpets, and he bites neighbors in their heels. He bit me; I still have that scar.

(Shows scar.)

I didn't get a rabies shot because when I saw him up close, I realized he was no werewolf, but a weirdo with a hairy back. My José has manners. He is well-trained. He won't hurt anyone in the neighborhood, at least during the daytime. He's very proud of his 'hood. Besides, I would be so embarrassed! I would just die. Those Chicanos hold such grudges. Like they say, "Chicano Alzheimer's." They forget everything but a grudge.

It's not easy raising kids nowadays, let alone a vampire *cholo* from hell. *(She starts to cry.)*

The Neighborhood Watch people have been complaining. They want to throw us out of the neighborhood. *Ay,* those Neighborhood Watch people. They're not so high and mighty. I saw Mr. Rodríguez neighborhood-watching me during my shower. *Cochino. (Loudly.)* Strike him dead, Lord! I know I need to look on the good side and be thankful. Why can't I have a kid like Cody, Kathy Lee's kid? You know that woman on the Regis and Kathy Lee Show? I'm trying. Let's see. *Déjame* ver. Ever since he became a vampire, he's had a sense of purpose. I thank God for that.

(She cries and then growling is heard.)

José, oh, Lord, not now. Chata, get behind La Lazy Boy. He's up and hungry. José, get back. Back! I say, Child of Darkness! *(She pulls out holy water and throws it on him. We hear screams and hisses off stage.)*

Get back Son of Darkness.

(Chanting.) "The stronger the Lord, the power is much stronger. I bring you from darkness to light." *(She pulls out a cross.)*

I don't like threatening him too often with the stake, sunlight and holy water, but it's tough love. *(We hear him whimpering. He has calmed down.)*

(To Chata.)

Ay, look at him. He's teething—that's why he's so cranky. I just think it's a phase.

(The BUZZING of a fly is heard. She swats at it, misses and pulls out a hymnal and swats it. We hear it fall to the ground. We hear a voice say "Help me! Help me!")

Ay! That fly has a head on it. It looks like Evelina's boy, the scientist. It's a sign. At least, my boy is whole. It could have been worse. *Ay,* I better put him in my coin purse. What a neighborhood we live in, Chata! Poor José, I know it's just a phase.

BLACK OUT.

7. SNAP OUT OF IT

Lights reveal a talk show stage. We hear the Larry Sanders' music theme and an announcer's voice. We see a blonde Latina dressed expensively with lots of clothes and jewelry. An effeminate male voice is heard.

ANNOUNCER: Welcome to "Talk To Me." Please give a big hand to our Lady of Self-Actualization and the producer and star of cable access' number one show, my sister Josephine Bautista.

JOSEPHINE: *(Turns to him.)* Thank you, Danny. Welcome to "Talk to Me." Talk to me. Don't be embarrassed. I want to help you. Whatever your sexual or emotional troubles, I can fix them.

I did one thousand hours of observational study with Oprah Winfrey. And I have had more guests killed on my show than Jenny Jones. I have cured many Latino problems: Banda Compulsives, Piñata envy, Argentineans with an irrational fear of not being European. I have worked hard on myself. I was a Cuban with low self-esteem. Do you know how rare that is? It's very rare.

I've also cured some Central Americans with the humility syndrome. When I think of that poor valet-parking attendant with a Cadillac on his foot, waiting for the customer to return. It really breaks my heart.

Now I want you to get help. As I say in my controversial book, *"Coño,* You Just Don't Understand!" or the classic "Women who Run with Chihuahuas," or in my best seller, "Women Are from Venus and Men Are From Tijuana."

I got well. Why can't you? I'm going to use one of my most controversial techniques. It is called "Snap Out of It." Now I'm going to use one of my servants. José is going to volunteer or look for a new job. Good José.

(To José.)

José, are you becoming a paranoid schizophrenic because you believe that men in green suits are trying to deport you back to Mexico around payday? Well?

(Screams.)

Snap out of it!

Do you think proposition one eighty-seven is just for Latinos? Hmm? Well?

(Screams.)

Snap out of it!

Do you believe I'm a bitch because I make my help be on my show for free, huh? Well?

(Screams.)

Snap out of it! Break through. Good. Give yourself a hand. Therapy is a wise investment. Therapy's not cheap. I do one-on-one counseling. I don't do group therapy.

(Beat.)

I had a bad experience with a gang from East L.A. They were totally enmeshed. Their inner children jumped me. There were ten of them, not counting multiple personalities. It took me a month to get all the writing off my couch.

(Throw away.) Damn those magic markers.

(Condescending.) I know worrying about food and money can be stressful, but I never went to Europe after my graduation and I was the only Latina at Swarthmore. Oh, that was painful. I got to work through this. So we've all suffered, Okay!

Let's deal with your real problems. How do you feel about your parents? Anyone? I'll share. I can't stand mine. My parents were really bugging me. I came this close to developing Menéndez Brothers Syndrome. I bought my mother a bull's-eye apron for Christmas and got my Daddy a neat deer-antler hat. I told him to prance in the backyard while Mr. Rifle Scope looked for him. Why didn't you love me Daddy? I'm lovable.

(Still agitated.)

Good, I had a breakthrough. Now you need one. Were you ever beaten? The police don't count. I'm talking about real oppression. Did your parents beat you with a belt?

(Painful.)

Mine had more subtle ways. They made me go to piñata parties. I had an out-of-body experience when I got hit by a baseball bat at a piñata party.

(Angrily.)

Piñatas. That's a great idea. Thanks, Eduardo and María. Let's blindfold a kid and put him in the middle of a bunch of defenseless kids, spin him around and let him swing a bat wildly around. Why don't you just buy the kid a chainsaw?

(She cries and throws herself on the ground.) Oh God, I hurt. But therapy has got me well. Wow, that was good.

(Smiling.)

What's wrong? Tell me. Talk to me. I don't have all night. This is all the air time my parents will pay for. They won't ever just let me be a self-actualized Latina without totally enmeshing me in a Jungian web of manipulation and deceit. When I said that to them, they just looked at me like I was crazy. Talk to me people. I'm not getting any calls. Therapy for Latinos really works. Let's break the ice.

Latinas, have you threatened to cut your man's dick off? I want to see a show of hands. I know I'm not alone.

Oh, us Latinas have been doing it for years. Only John Wayne Bobbitt reported it. No self-respecting Latino male would report that. If a Latino man gets his dick cut off, he won't tell anybody. He'll be in the back yard with a flashlight looking around with his buddy, saying, "I lost something back here. Wait. Don't touch that. Oh, never mind, it's a garden hose."

All right then, I'm the only one with that problem. It's denial, ladies. Fine. Who needs you bitches?

(Angry then remorseful.) Oh God, now you won't like me. *(Desperate.)* Hold me! *(She breaks down crying.)*

I feel so close to you all. Like we're all family, except no one is cursing in Spanish at me. I want to share with you that psychology. It all adds up to this: We all want to be loved, but we want to be loved for us. Just us, the way our parents loved us when we were first born, or how we imagine God must love us. And we want to tell our story, to be understood, to be heard.

(She turns backstage and screams.) Mom, I'm talking right now. I'm doing my talk show. I'll release the servants in a minute. *(She turns back to the audience.)*

Don't you even dare move. José, María, sit down. *Siéntense.* As I was saying, we want to be loved and understood, but no one really does so. We don't find it and we end up visiting a psychologist. You end up visiting me, wondering if I'm the answer.

But I want you to know, I care. I really care just about you, and I accept you unconditionally.

(Lovingly caring.) I care. I want you to know that I really care. I really can't tell you how much I care till next week, because we're out of time. But I care. Remember, Latinos, you can be happy living in America if you do one little thing for me: Snap out of it! God, therapy feels good.

FADE OUT.

8. METRICALLY CHALLENGED

A classic Spanish tune, "Granada," is heard. A matador enters. The lights reveal a man in tights with a large belly. He is fat. He holds a garment bag and sucks on an asthma respirator. He is eating a donut. He appears winded as he quickly runs in. He speaks with a theta Spanish lisp.

FAT MATADOR: I'm sorry. I'm sorry I'm late, but the bakery did not open till 10 A.M. *(He pulls out child-size matador outfit from his garment bag.)* Oh, my God, who shrunk my tights? Juan, someone has shrunk my shorts. Oh, my God, they are definitely smaller. Just before the end of the season, they are trying to get rid of me. I know it. I was the best, but lately, well, the last ten years, I have had troubles. I feel I have a case. They want to hire a skinny matador with no qualifications. It's this quota system. It's affirmative action. They have to hire skinny matadors and forget better-qualified fat matadors. They say I'm metrically challenged by about a 100 kilos. They say that I should run with the Bulls of Pamplona three times a week before I ever fight again. It's a quota system. They have to hire so many skinny matadors. Guys like me just don't have a chance. But it's not my fault, these bulls are just too fast. What have they been feeding them lately? I swear to God, these bulls are sponsored by Nike.

I miss the old days when my suits fit and there wasn't this constant perfectionist ideal about beauty. My God, I feel like Elvis during the Vegas years. But I said to them, he used to pack them in, and so can I!

Right now, I've got to pack myself in these shorts. We need to redefine how a matador should look. I'm not fat; I'm stocky. I have big bones.

Was Oprah Winfrey less worthwhile when she was fat? Was Orson Wells less of a director? Was Shamu less of a whale? No. Stop the insanity!!!

I know they want to fire me. You have to help me. I know the signs: they mock me, they no longer send fried foods to my room. Someone sent up some Jenny Craig *paella* light! That was the bulimic matador from Bolivia. That's got to be harassment. Sue the bastards.

I can take a hint. Why all these celery sticks? What kind of disrespect is this? I came this close to getting that Madonna video.

I feel great, except for the high blood pressure and lower back pains. I can do my job.

(To an audience member.)

You try to wear a little suit and go against a big angry side of beef that doesn't want to be *carne asada*. It's craziness. But bull fighting is all I know. The bulls are improving. Why can't we? *(He takes a gun out of his plastic garment bag.)*

I'm packing, god damn it. I've got a gun. I don't care if the people boo me. Screw it. I am a modern bullfighter. I am redefining this sport. They can't fire me. *(Beat.)*

Oh, hell with it. I'm nervous. I need some Hagen Daaz and a *paella* and some good ham and some calamari and bread and some good Andalucian salami and a diet coke. *(He takes a whiff out of the Primatene.)*

I used to be so great, but you try doing this for years and you start to dream of bulls, bulls, bulls, always the horns. I see them. Those angry bulls wanting their hoofs and ears back. I want to be a vegetarian but I like barbecue too much, and pie and Cheetos. Well, maybe I could stand to lose a little weight. Maybe I can lose just a little weight. Maybe I can have two shakes and a sensible nine-course meal, and maybe buy a juicer. Yes, I can juice the donuts in the morning. Hell, with that—I got rights. I'm not changing. I got seniority. I know I have a case.

It's affirmative action. They got this quota system that forces the owners to hire anorexic matadors. But it's not my fault. I tell you these bulls are just too damn fast. Do I have a case? I have a case of Cheetos. *I'm hungry.*

(Yells out of the window.)

I'm telling you. It's not my fault. These bulls are just too damn fast. They can't fire me. They can't fire me...

BLACK OUT.

9. YOU KNOW HOW TO WHISTLE, DON'T YOU?

(This piece was written for and dedicated to Charo Toledo.)

An innocent-looking young attractive Latina comes out in a faded '50's dress. Her hair is disheveled. She is trying to look like a '40's movie actress, but faded. She is barefoot. Her feet are dirty. She whistles in the darkness as the lights come up.

CUBA LIBRE: If you want me, just whistle. You know how to whistle, don't you? You just put your lips together and blow.

I've seen the movie one hundred million times!

(Coy.)

Oh, I shouldn't say a million; I'm a good communist.

(Fact.)

You have dollars. I bet you got a million.

(Pleading.)

Don't turn away. Wait. Don't go away. I see it in your eyes. Don't turn away. Don't think your thoughts. I hear them. They hurt me, they whip me.

(Serious.)

Life is tough here. I sell myself to tourists for dollars to provide for my mother...

(Faking it.)... who is sick, uh, with some tropical disease. Without dollars, you die.

There is no more life in Cuba. I do what I have to survive...

Wait, don't go. *(Astonished.)*

Oh my God, you're unmoved. You must be an American. You have a cold heart. I could warm it.

(Seductively.)

I could defrost that cold heart. I could warm it within my tropical borders and save your life, teach you to love. I could defrost your heart like a microwave oven, cleanly, gently, economically, efficiently. *(Seductively rolls her tongue around the mouth.)*

Efficiently. Would you like that?

(Plainly.) I can be a nice girl and sit in your lap. We can play spin the rum bottle. And if you're a *marica* boy and you don't like girls, that's okay. We can talk about Judy Garland. But if you do like girls, then prove it, rent a room.

Oh wait, maybe you have a little pito, like when you get naked, girls say, "Oh, how cute, two belly buttons."

Wait. I could be your tour guide here in Havana. You like Cuban architecture? You like my architecture? My big Latin arches? I have a strongly influenced African culture that is aching for your New England colonial influence to drive me mad with envy and desire.

(Realizing.) You don't like me? I bore you? I'm ugly? Fat? Why don't you like me? You don't want me? You led me on, you bastard!

(Angrily.) I gave myself to you. I loved you.

(Weeps.) Go ahead, leave me. Tear out my heart and boil it.

(Threatening.) Okay. You, want trouble. I'll call La Guardia right now and say you tried to rape me. Maybe say you were saying shit about Castro. That you were saying he is an old man with an ugly beard. Oh, he hates that. You don't know what life is till you watch it leave you in a Cuban jail.

(Angrily and fast.) Coño, carajo, puñeta, no puedo creer que yo todavía estoy hablando con este hombre. Wait. I'm not angry. I'm just Caribbean.

All right.

(Business-like.) I could do translations for you. I can speak three different languages and type ten words per minute.

(Like a drone.) This plaza is where Castro plotted with Che, right here in this coffee shop. And over there is where my parents met; they sipped coffee here with an escort, a chaperone. And people stood on those balconies and watched the sunset and applauded the particularly good ones. People sipped... *(Remembering.)*

People sipped... *Cuba libre here. Cuba libre means free Cuba.* Free Cuba, *Cuba libre.*

(Beat, simply, dropping the act.)

Oh fuck it, rent a room. I'll lie with you for free.

(Slowly.)

No dollars, free. I just want to imagine I'm in California with the Hollywood sign behind us and a full moon. And we'll make love in your beautiful home with all the lights on and the windows open.

And there will be no shame because I'll be your bride and you'll be my husband. We'll make love not in secret. And I'll lie in your arms. I'll be happy and never dream of Cuba. Rent a room. I'll lie with you for free. At least, I'll be off this island. I'll be off this island for just one moment, even if it's just in my mind.

You can have me for free. I can set you free. You can fuck me for free. *Cuba libre. Cuba libre.*

BLACK OUT.

Mexican Moses comes out. He now has transformed. His beard is all white and so is his hair. There are two rays of light coming from his head. They look like horns. He comes out holding the commandments. They are engraved on a velvet painting

MEXICAN MOSES: God has turned me into Freddie Fender, man can he talk! Okay, I got them. Here are ten commandments for us Latinos:

First, though shall be on time. Stop grumbling, just set your watches an hour early... two hours in the case of Chicanos, you know its true. Stop your grumbling.

Second, though shalt love your fellow Latino as yourself. And I don't want that to be an excuse to love your fellow Latinas, and I mean we must love all of us despite our diffcrences and love... *(Hard for him to say this.)* Lord you're testing me... love Argentinians.

Thirdly, though shall not covet or want what your other Latino brother or sister has. His success.

Fourthly... where was I? I had them memorized. Oh, yes. His car and only his car. I think we know who we're talking to. They're from East Los Angeles and Forty-Second. I want my car back.

Oh yes, fifth, turn both your cheecks to Anglos and tell them to kiss them. No, that's a typo. Be kind to everyone: Latino, Anglo, Asian, man, woman, child and animal, because it's right. Because if you don't, he gets really mad. He's not threatening to kill you. That's old style. He's threatening to let you live in a really miserable world with a lot of people as cruel and as miserable as you. No, not New York. He'll let you live right where you are and that's not pretty, so change your ways.

Seventh, I know I skipped one. The German Moses wanted more commandments, so he gave them a couple of yours. I don't know what they're going to do with some *piñata* commandments, look no further than your mirror.

He really wants you to learn to turn in your weapons and exchange them for tickets to Disneyland, but, well, the N.R.A. has this lobby in heaven that really got some pull.

Eighth. No more petty bickering or divisions. Look how to build a future together; be a tribe, a family, a nation.

Ninth, you can call yourself anything you want: Mexican of American descent, Chicano, Latino, Hispanic, Brown or, I like this, the Children of the Sun.—But that's long. Or you can just call yourself plain American. Call yourself anything you want 'cause a name's just a word. Call a gun a flower; it's still s gun. Your actions will define you and that's it.

When we started this journey, the Anglos were really helpful; especially Pete Wilson. He called and the whole Republican party donated buses to help us to leave. And we wandered here to Bakersfield. But I'm disbanding you all. Oh, I'm disbanding this walk back to Aztlán, or mythical Mexico, because it doesn't exist. It's not on the map. We didn't feel we belonged, like we were an invited guest at a wedding.

Well, tenth, this is the biggest commandment. Though shalt know that you belong. This is the promised land, the land flowing with milk and kahlua. We all belong. And you don't have to take it to know it's yours. You tell them Mexican Moses told you it was yours; it was ordained. Everyone who hears my voice—Black, Anglo, Asian, Latino, Native American—you belong. This is yours. Welcome home. This is your promised land.

BLACK OUT.

A QUIET LOVE

Note:

This play was originally commissioned by San Diego Reperatory Theater under the direction of Doug Jacobs. All characters mentioned in this play are loosely based on my family. The dialogue is fictional.

This play is dedicated to Mary Ubale Najera, who taught me the meaning of the title of this play.

A QUIET LOVE

A Quiet Love is a cross generation story of the Najera clan. The show has a lot of characters that can be performed by six actors, each portraying multiple roles. The characters are:

Ed Najera/Chon/Young Ed: a good-looking tall, Mexican man in his forties to play a range of ages from twenties to sixties.

Mary Najera/Josefina/Young Mary: a good-looking Mexican-American woman, late thirties to play a range of ages from early twenties to fifties.

Rick Najera/Sailor/Man: Mexican-American man, age twenty-eight.

Sophie/Doctor/Cherie Grizzeled Worker: a Mexican-American woman who plays a range of ages from early twenties to fifty.

Union Officer/Marlo/White Slaver/Steve/Foreman/Captain: a white man in his late thirties.

Andy/Black Guy/Officer/Sailor #1/Louie Canado: a man in his late thirties.

The staging of the play should be minimal. The furniture simple and functional, with no particular time period attached, i.e. benches, chairs, wood tables in the Shaker style. The staging will rely heavily on the back screen where slides about the family and slides marking the time period will be displayed.

PROLOGUE.

A young man / Rick walks on stage. He holds a cellular phone. On the other side of the stage appears another man / Andy, actor #2, also holding a cellular phone. They both talk with their backs to each other.

ANDY: Hey, how you doing? Uh, listen, they like you at Warner Brothers. But they think you're not ethnic enough. They wanted you to be more ethnic.

RICK: Would a burro and bandanna have helped? She said I was lucky to have such an interesting background.

ANDY: That's what she says to you. To me, she said, "They wanted you to be more ethnic."

RICK: What about CBS?

ANDY: They love you, but you're a little too ethnic for them. But they still loved you.

RICK: I'd rather have them hire me than love me. Am I up for any other shows?

ANDY: Well, uh. Uh. Well, there's no show with your special voice. But I'm on top of it.

RICK: My special ethnic voice. Let me tell you a little story. I was on a plane and a stewardess came up to me and said, "Mr. Najera, Mr. Najera, this Mexican man needs your help. Can you speak to him in your best Spanish possible?" I said, "Sure." So I walked up to him and said, *(Accent.)* "Chew are going ta die."

ANDY: Is that a true story?

RICK: No, it's a joke and so is Hollywood. I just want to work, Andy.

ANDY: You'll work. There's just no show that needs your kind of talent at the moment. I got another call. Listen, there's one more show that's still hiring. I'm going to get an answer by the end of the day. Where can I reach you?

RICK: In San Diego. See ya.

END OF PROLOGUE.

BLACK OUT.

Scene 1

Sound of a beautiful corrido fills the air. It is called "Un amor callado," A Quiet Love. The lights reveal a man sitting on a Lazy Boy recliner holding a hot water bottle to his throat. A woman adjusts a pillow and brings him a cup of water. On stage stands a lone figure.

RICK: Sight is deceptive. We are surrounded by optical illusions. When you see the moon low on the horizon, it appears much larger, but if it's high on the horizon, it seems much smaller. The moon hasn't changed its size. It's our senses that are wrong. Our own sight cannot be trusted. His is failing. *(Ed reaches for his glasses and picks up a book.)*

I see a sick old man. I see an old man in quiet agony, but I know he's really a giant. My mother brings him a cool drink. She's a giant, too. We cannot always trust our sight or our memories. Most things I forget. I blame it on my generation's lack of strong genes. I think the lack of the ozone layer, the constant bombardment of gamma rays and TV rays and consumption of twinkies, have made us a weaker generation. Of course, this is just my perception and perceptions can be wrong.

I'm telling this story because if I don't write it down, if I don't record it, I'll forget it. And I don't want to forget. He'll remember because he has an incredible memory. That's one of the reasons he's a giant and I'm his son—he'll remember. *(Lights change and Ed speaks.)*

ED: Mary, would you bring me one of my shakes?

MARY: Eddie, you need to eat some solid food, not just shakes. Now, come on.

RICK: It's what we remember. It's important. It's our own stories that are the true history. We must listen to learn. *(He turns to his father.)* Dad, I want to record you.

ED: I lost my butt this morning. I looked in the mirror and I swear to God I had no butt. This book on World War II is very good.

RICK: Dad, I want to record you.

MARY: You don't want to write about us—we're not interesting. You've got a good imagination. Why don't you write about interesting people? Did you see the Elizabeth Taylor Story? She's interesting. She just keeps getting more and more interesting.

ED: And bigger.

MARY: Don't mention that "chicken feet in the soup" thing. I'll hear about it from Sophie for days.

RICK: All I said was that I remember chicken feet in my grandfather's soup. The reporter wrote down what he heard.

ED: Why'd he say you grew up in a barrio?

RICK: I guess that's what he heard. I told him I grew up in Barrio La Mesa.

MARY: Oh, God, Sophie was so mad. She said, "It made us sound poor. Chicken feet in our soup."

ED: There was chicken feet in the caldo. It made the soup taste better. But they were clean chickens, free range.

MARY: Why talk about us? We're not interesting. And don't say you were in the barrio. I took you out of the barrio. Your dad would have stayed in the barrio.

ED: I liked the barrio. My family and friends were there. Barrio just meant neighborhood. Beverly Hills is a barrio and they don't call 'em gangs. They call 'em fraternities.

MARY: How's things going in L.A?

RICK: Great.

MARY: I got "Call Waiting." I got "Call Waiting." I know how nervous you get if you don't hear from your agent. How's L.A.? Are you safe there?

RICK: I feel safer in San Diego. Surrounded by the military. You have battleships and jets all over the place. Just driving here, I saw a tank on the side of the road. This place is armed to the teeth. Who are we fighting?

ED: No one, that's why your brother is unemployed.

MARY: "Call Waiting" is such a pain.

RICK: I just don't like it when someone's on the phone while I'm expecting a call.

MARY: I been reading *Variety.*

RICK: Do you subscribe to *Variety?*

MARY: You've got to keep up with the industry. And *Buzz Magazine.* I like *Buzz.*

STEVE: *(Steve enters. He is a mysterious quiet man, reading a book and eating a sandwich. The role of Steve is also actor #1.)* The military has kept this town alive. The Berlin Wall falling was not a good thing. I know things, Rick.

RICK: Well you don't know how to get a job.

STEVE: After my retraining, I'll be able to get a job in the private sector.

RICK: Sure, you can give them fries or espionage.

STEVE: You don't know what I did.

RICK: Tell me while my recorder is on.

STEVE: I'm going out. *(Steve exits.)*

RICK: *(To Ed.)* All right, the recorder's on. What is your earliest memory?

ED: I remember the *Virgin de Guadalupe Church.* We lived
across the street from it. *(We see a slide of the church in
the back wall.)*

RICK: There's a freeway across from the church.

ED: I was there, and there used to be a house. It was my
father's house. The first Mexicans in Logan Heights. He
created a barrio.

RICK: Oh, yeah, that's going to make Anglos real happy. The
first Mexicans in Logan Heights. There's some guy saying,
"If only we could go back in time and stop that lone Mexican man... Logan Heights would be the country club it
was meant to be."

ED: But he didn't look Mexican. He was tall with blue eyes.
Look at this picture. That's him as a young man. He came
to this country when he was just a baby. That was around
1898. *(On a screen behind them appears a picture of Chon
Najera. Lights change, the slide says Chihuahua, Mexico.)*

RICK: Why'd they leave?

ED: They owned some stores, and one of the uncles had
kicked a lone little peasant out of the store. He suspected
him of shoplifting. That peasant was Pancho Villa. You
know how Mexicans hold grudges.

RICK: Is that true?

ED: Write it down, let them decide. The reason they came
here is too boring to write down.

RICK: How'd my great-grandmother die?

ED: Lifting a hog.

RICK: Big woman.

ED: Bigger hog.

RICK: How'd my great-grandfather die?

ED: Old age.

RICK: Great-great-grandmother?

ED: Childbirth.

RICK: Great-great-grandfather?

ED: Old age.

RICK: I'm seeing a pattern. Great-great-great-grandfather? How was he killed?

ED: Cortez. My grandfather moved from Chihuahua, Mexico, to Alamo Gordo, which became the test site of the nuclear bomb. Yeah, my grandfather moved to New Mexico, bought a ranch and started a new business. That's where your grandfather met your grandmother, in your great-grandfather's store.

RICK: Wasn't there an uncle of mine who stayed back there in Chihuahua?

ED: Yeah, sure. Lots of family stayed.

MARY: You probably have Spanish-speaking cousins over there.

ED: But you won't be able to talk to them. Back then, New Mexico was just a different part of Mexico.

RICK: I'm starting to feel the same way about L.A.

ED: If the original Mexican border patrol stopped more Anglos, this would still be Mexico. *(Laughs.)*

RICK: That's my joke.

ED: I think my father had dual citizenship, and I know my mother was already an American citizen because her brother went to World War I.

RICK: How'd he die?

ED: Mustard gassed by the Germans. Your grandfather then left New Mexico.

RICK: Why?

ED: There was this land dispute when your great-grandfather Manuel died. They gave your grandfather a rifle and a ticket to California and told him he had no land. That was the condition for him to sign the papers.

RICK: What papers?

ED: The papers to give away his share of land.

RICK: Why did he give his share of land away?

ED: Because he didn't want to fight his brothers for it. Besides, the government confiscated most of the land to make a nuclear test site.

RICK: So his freedom meant more to him than the land?

ED: Yes, he was free to go to California.

RICK: Did my grandmother go with him?

ED: No, he worked at the Hotel Del Coronado as a dishwasher, saved up money and then sent for her.

RICK: How did Tata end up in Logan Heights?

ED: The landlord of the house wanted to rent, but didn't know your grandfather was Mexican, he was so light and tall. It was after they had already signed the lease and your grandmother arrived, when he realized that the first Mexicans had arrived.

RICK: Right, because my Nana was dark and part Apache.

ED: There were blacks in Logan Heights, too, and Japanese. Well, they were there, but they got deported to Manzanar. And there was a German couple who lived next door. They were all good people.

RICK: Yeah, why didn't they deport the Germans during the war?

MARY: Rick, you got to stop and think. With the Germans, you knew what they were thinking. The Japanese have always been inscrutable.

RICK: Well, they own Hawaii, so they won't bomb it anymore.

ED: I knew a Japanese girl, Sumiko. She got deported. One minute we were calling them neighbors, the next minute we were calling them Japs. I need to work on that bathroom tomorrow. It's almost finished.

RICK: Do you realize that they built the Coronado Bay Bridge faster?

ED: Well, my bathroom will last longer. I know at least the tile on that shower will take the test of time. The Mayans had the pyramids to point to. I have the tile.

MARY: How's L.A.?

RICK: It's just great. Earthquakes, fires, riots. I'm waiting for Godzilla to walk down Hollywood Blvd.

ED: Does it get cold in L.A.? I've got a coat for you. It's my favorite coat.

RICK: Yeah, Dad, it gets cold. Uh... Thanks... (Ed starts to cough.) I wonder if your throat problems come from agent orange. Maybe you can sue the government.

MARY: Rick, the government's trying to help you. Why do you have to make the government look like bad people? You're sounding so bitter. Try to be nice.

RICK: What do you remember?

ED: I remember to take my medicine nowadays, and that's about it.

RICK: No, Dad, I mean about our family. Did you ever meet your great-grandfather?

ED: Your great-great-grandfather came to Mexico from Spain when he was thirteen. You might be related to Gutiérrez Najera, the poet. Your grandfather was a poet, too.

MARY: I saved one of his poems. *(Mary hands it to Rick.)*

RICK: "Like a feather wafting down from an eagle's flight; something I learned before they kicked me out of school." That is beautiful and ironic.

MARY: It's not ironic. They kicked him out of school in the third grade.

ED: It is ironic. Do you know what irony is? They did not kick him out of school. He left. But his father's father moved from Mexico City to Chihuahua, Mexico, because they owned some stores there. But when the Revolution came, they moved to New Mexico.

RICK: That's where my grandfather was raised, right?

ED: That's where he met your grandmother. She was part Apache. That's where she got her toughness. She once set her own leg when it was broken. She was tough.

RICK: That explains her gentle demeanor.

MARY: That was sarcasm. I know what irony means. I'm not stupid. You are getting so mean in your old age, which is *ironic* because you used to be so nice. I'm going to get the last word, Eddy. Women always do.

ED: Your grandfather came to work at the Hotel Del Coronado so that he could save up enough money to bring her over from New Mexico. He worked as a dishwasher.

MARY: Isn't it ironic that his grandson Johnny works at Hotel Del?

RICK: It is. His name is John and my grandfather's name was Chon.

ED: John is a banquet captain. Chon was a dishwasher. After three generations, we have now moved from dishwasher to banquet captain.

RICK: Kinda makes you get all misty. Huh?

ED: Well, that's how it works. First generation dishwasher, second generation busboy, third generation waiter. It's cultural evolution.

MARY: Don't feel sorry for Johnny. He gets tips. But he always reports them. Be sure to write that down.

ED: He loved to go to Tijuana with your grandmother and party all night.

STEVE: *(Steve enters with* Time *magazine.)* I don't want you to write about me.

RICK: I don't know anything about you, just that you worked in intelligence all around the world.

STEVE: Maybe. There's an article in *Time* magazine about someone like me. You'll notice a magazine with a water stain. *(Holds up five fingers.)* Read it, you'll figure out what I did. *(Steve leaves.)*

RICK: God, he's spooky.

MARY: Leave him alone. He's out of work. No one needs to know what he used to do. He was so much more secure when the Russians were in power.

RICK: We'll find another enemy.

MARY: Your grandparents were fun people to party with. They loved mariachis and drinking. They would never take care of the grandchildren. She'd say to Eddie, "you had them, you take 'em."

ED: *(To Rick.)* She was very *terca*, stubborn.

MARY: She ran that house and your grandfather with an iron fist. Once, your grandmother Nana was mad at your father, and she told Chon that he couldn't really visit us. Once Chon wanted to give us some tamales, so he wrapped them up and sent them by mail. And we only lived three blocks away.

ED: *(To Rick.)* It's a shame you never really knew her. They loved each other, without boundaries. He loved her for seventy years.

RICK: They were totally enmeshed. That's a psychological term.

ED: Oh, yeah, they were enmeshed, enraged, battered, bruised. They were a lot of things.

MARY: One time your father gave her stewed tomatoes to his roosters.

ED: She tried to kill him with a frying pan. She complained, saying that he bruised her arm trying to hold her back from hitting him.

MARY: It was a real thick frying pan.

ED: You're making her sound bad. She hit him with a frying pan. But it was a light one. He raised fighting cocks and went to jail for it, jail or a fifty dollar fine. He needed the money to pay a midwife for my birth, so he went to jail. He used to believe you could raise a rooster through the bloodlines. He would watch the roosters carefully to see which would breed the best offspring.

RICK: That's how he watched me. One time, he put two roosters together to fight, but he wasn't watching the roosters. He was watching me watching the roosters. I don't know what he was looking for.

ED: He was watching you to see if you saw what he saw.

RICK: The war? Why'd you go? *(Old 1940s Mexican music plays. It's subtle in the background.)*

ED: I'm an American. If there's a war, I should fight.

RICK: Was that the real reason you went? Because you loved America?

ED: Yeah, well the real reason was that I wanted a going-
away party. I liked getting up on a chair and making
speeches. I felt important. Everyone was getting a going-
away party and they were great. There were the big
bands Count Basey and Dorsey. It was a great time...
they made the war seem glamorous. Hollywood made it
look great. As an American, I liked the idea of a star in
our window. I had been reading this book about what I
did in the war. *(We see a photo of a star in the window
fading into a slide saying "Battleship U.S. Missouri 1943."
We see the ensemble of actors dressed as marines. They are
practicing a drill, attacking one another. We see a Navy
captain played by actor #1. A Navy captain's voice is
heard.)*

CAPTAIN: Everyone line up in rows of three. *(Old Ed
becomes young Ed. He lines up in the front of one of the
lines. Going to Ed.)* Since you are first in line, I see that
you have initiative. You are in charge of the men behind
you. One will be your mechanic, one will be in charge of
communications and the machine gun. That is your landing craft. You will take that landing craft and drive it up
to a beach. Men will try to kill you. You will take men on
the landing craft and deposit them on land. I repeat, men
will try to kill you. Then you will sail back to the mother
ship. While you're sailing back to the mother ship, men
will try to kill you. You will do that as many times as you
can until someone kills you. If no one kills you, you will go
to another battle where someone will try to kill you. Do
you have any questions?

ED: What if no one kills me?

CAPTAIN: The Navy has not planned for that to happen. As
for the Indians on this ship, you will all be scouts. You
can follow tank tracks, can't you? There you go, Cochese,
it's in your genes, so don't fight it.

CAPTAIN: Tex, you will follow Najera there, which is a great
irony. *(A slide projector flashes in black and white.*

"Tarawa, Pacific Ocean 1943." We see the ensemble of actors in Navy uniforms running for cover. We hear loud bombing noises.)

ED: Get them off the goddamn ship! Get them off! This is low tide. We can't land on low tide.

SAILOR/ACTOR #2: Who's in charge?

ED: I am. This is my ship. Start swimming.

SAILOR/ACTOR #2: Who made you God?

ED: The United States Navy, the same guys that came up with the brilliant idea of landing on low tide. Now move it!

SAILOR/ACTOR #2: They're all off the ship. Let's get the hell out of here.

ED: We got to come back? this is just the first trip.

SAILOR/ACTOR #2: We got to go back? Are you crazy?

ED: Not yet, but I'm getting close. I'm going to get that wounded man on the ship. Hey, they're shooting their Jap prisoners. Anyone tries this on this ship, you gun them down. Got that, Tex?

SAILOR/ACTOR #2: I ain't going to shoot an American.

ED: Just the bad ones. I'm going to get that man. *(There is a big explosion. Ed gets buried underneath sand. Blackout. The stage becomes eerily silent. We hear digging. Then we hear Ed's voice as he tries to dig himself out of the sand.)* I was buried. I couldn't breathe. I was digging. I was digging north, south... I didn't know. The explosion had buried me underneath the sand. I couldn't breathe. I was buried but I wasn't dead. Yet, I was buried. Then I could breathe. It was like being born again. *(Lights slowly reveal Ed sitting in the Lazy Boy chair. We go back to Rick in the present time.)* I dug myself out. I fought for life. I guess I came close to feeling birth and death at the same time. I can't stand being in closed spaces. Never let them bury me. You understand? When I die, cremate me, spread my ashes at sea and just remember me.

RICK: You're not going to die for a long time. You'll outlive us all. Goddamn it, stop talking about that. *(Changes subject.)* Uh. Were there a lot of Latinos in the war?

ED: More Latinos have silver stars than any other group. Your cousin, Joe Galindo, has a silver star. I should have gotten a purple heart.

RICK: Did you ever get that purple heart?

ED: No, I didn't come home with a purple heart. I came home with claustrophobia and shrapnel. Let's stop for a minute—my throat hurts. Mary, could you get me another shake? *(He coughs.)*

RICK: You want to go outside? You want to go to the movies?

ED: No, too many germs. They got that flesh-eating bacteria running around.

RICK: I saw this guy on the news. The flesh-eating bacteria ate part of him. Ate away about thirty pounds of him—he looked great. Fit into pants he hadn't worn since his college days. *(Bringing out Ed's shake.)*

MARY: Maybe if that flesh-eating bacteria caught Steve, in three years he would be wearing his senior prom suit. Don't tell anyone I said that. God's going to punish me.

ED: *(To Rick.)* Let's go outside. Maybe we'll find some mint and make some tea. *(Enters, looks at the empty stage. Goes to the tape recorder and turns it on.)*

STEVE: Flesh-eating bacteria, strange coincidence weird diseases, page forty-two in this national best seller explains what's really going on. No government agency is going to refute it. If they try and stop the book, it would give the book too much validation. It might cause a panic. In the middle of the first chapter, there's a major clue about what's really going on here. This book is not fiction. It's the truth, it's a fact. Page forty-two, it explains all. Rick, you want stories that have completion. You won't find that in real life. You won't find it here... *(He hears Mary walking in. He puts down the recorder and leaves. They exit. Mary walks in and sits down in her chair. She is cut-*

ting coupons from the newspaper. She looks around and speaks into the tape recorder.)

MARY: I have a little story about the war. I know if you're going to write a story, war stories are the most interesting. My brother went to war. To the Philippines. We were living in Iowa, in Boone, Iowa. My parents chose Boone because in Texas, they didn't treat Mexicans good. They were from Aguas calientes *(Hot Waters)*. The weather was hot, the water was hot, everything was hot. Then they came to Iowa, where everything was cold: the water was cold, the weather was cold, everything was cold. People used to always give me advice. The nuns at my school, they said to me, "Never share your clothes with boys, because it could get you pregnant. Only sit on a boy's lap if there's a telephone book between you." And, you know, they were right.

My brother was the only one who didn't advise me. He just listened to me. He was voted best dressed in school, and he had only two shirts. He would iron them and keep his clothes so clean. He took me to see Al Jolson in the movie *California Here I Come.* Once Al Jolson sang "California here I Come," I knew that's where I'd be going. So at fifteen, I left for California. A man asked me, "Where are you going?" And I said, "I'm an Indian princess from the reservation and I'm going to California."

My brother was much older than me. He already was in the Air Force, in the Philippines. He used to send all his money home. I got a letter of his. He said, "I saw a sunset today. It made me realize how small I am and how great God is." IIe was captured in the Philippines when he was on the Bataan Death March. He was forced to march with sixty thousand other soldiers from Bataan. Six thousand died along the way, because they had no water or food. He survived it and was put in a Japanese concentration camp.

He wanted to be a pilot. One of the survivors said one day he was watching some Zeroes warming up. He said he planned to steal one. He said he knew he could fly. But before he could escape... just before he was liberated, just before that... the Japanese put him and others in a pit, poured in gasoline and lit them all on fire. He was seventeen. He was so young. I wonder if he was looking up at the sky, if he was thinking of flying away. And just to think that if only the Japanese had waited another day, my brother would still be alive. Only one day more and he would have been free.

I don't understand. Well, God only knows, but it sometimes makes me mad. If you stop and think what great things he could have done!

My sister asked a man who was a survivor of that concentration camp if he knew my brother. See, this soldier had memorized everyone's name in the camp. At first, he didn't remember Joe, but when my sister told him his full name, Joe Uballe, the man finally remembered. He remembered my brother's name after forty years! Isn't that something?

If you ever write about him, remember his name: Joe Uballe. That was his name. History forgets names, but please remember his name, Joe Uballe. *(Cries.)* I don't know if you should tell this story. Damn, think of nice stories, Rick.

ED: *(Offstage voice.)* Mary, come out here. Could you get me a shake?

MARY: I got it right here, Eddie. I want you to try and eat solid food, Eddie. *(She turns off the tape recorder. Rick enters.)*

RICK: Where's Maggie?

MARY: At the vet. She'll be okay. I ran over her accidentally. I saw her in pain. I told Eddie to get the gun and shoot her.

ED: *(Yells from out back.)* Yeah, she wanted to kill Maggie. Luckily, cool heads prevailed.

RICK: Imagine how embarrassed you would have been.

MARY: I thought she was suffering. They do it to horses. But now Eddie says he doesn't want to complain. He says I'm trigger-happy, and if he's in pain I might put him to sleep.

ED: *(Laughs.)* Oh, yeah, you could have the last word, then, "Good night, Eddy." I won't even ask for an aspirin. *(Rick goes to the computer, sits down, puts on corrido music. Attacks the key boards like a piano virtuoso. Steve enters.)*

STEVE: Did they already pay you for this commission?

RICK: Yeah.

STEVE: Big mistake. *(Exits.)*

MARY: I subscribe to *Buzz* magazine, so I'll know what you are doing in L.A.

RICK: Wow, *Buzz* magazine. Soon you'll be wearing black and getting a nose ring. I've never been in *Buzz*, Mom.

MARY: No, but you better be soon. I'm not getting younger. I was hoping you would be paying for my retirement. Now I'll settle for a dishwasher.

RICK: So was I. You used to say, "When you make it, you'll buy me a house."

MARY: Oh, well, you don't have to worry about that.

RICK: Are you starting not to believe in me?

MARY: No. *(Sophie is seen. There's a knock at the door.)* Look who's here, Sophie! Now, Rick, be nice. Don't mention any writing.

SOPHIE: *(Enters. She is with her son Marlo—about thirty-five with a short haircut. He wears cowboy boots, jeans and gold chains.)* Hi, is Rick here? I saw his car, so nice.

MARY: He's down from L.A.

MARLO: Nice car.

RICK: Thanks. Dad's in the back. Hi, Aunt Sophie, how are you?

SOPHIE: Great. What are you doing here?

RICK: I'm writing a little show.

SOPHIE: About my family?

MARY: It's going to be nice, very complimentary. No chicken feet stories.

SOPHIE: No poverty. No gangs.

RICK: Just me in the Boy Scouts, although we did have bandanas. *(Ed enters.)*

SOPHIE: Buddy, you look so thin. Oh, my God!

ED: I lost my butt. Sit down.

MARY: You want coffee?

MARLO: Yeah, you doing okay up in L.A? If you ever need me to be a stunt man in one of your shows, I'm ready. *(Marlo pretends he's a policeman.)* Freeze, punk. I do Tae Kwon Do like Van Damme. I can do Jackie Chan style or Norris style.

RICK: Dad, what went wrong?

SOPHIE: He's a cowboy. He dips chewing tobacco. He's a cowboy now. *(Marlo does a two-step.)*

MARLO: That's in case you need someone who is a line dancer. I chew tobacco and go line dancing now. Marlo does a two-step.

RICK: That's a skill. Have you got a horse?

MARLO: No, but I got 260 horsepower out of my truck. That's the modern horse. I can rope and tractor pull for hours.

SOPHIE: Marlo, just rest. I got a headache. You're no cowboy. You don't even have a horse.

MARLO: A lot of cowboys don't have horses.

SOPHIE: Marlo! So you're doing a story about this family?

RICK: Yeah.

MARY: It will probably never be seen. Anyone want coffee?

SOPHIE: Were you just writing?

RICK: Yeah, but I was stuck. *(Innocently.)* Do you mind if I ask you some questions?

SOPHIE: Okay.

RICK: What was it like in the barrio?

SOPHIE: It was no barrio. It was a neighborhood. Logan Heights was nice. There were good people who lived there.

RICK: Barrio is not a bad word. It just means neighborhood, like Mr. Roger's neighborhood. Who lived there?

SOPHIE: There was the black family—they were good. But they didn't tell anyone they were black. They said they were Cuban. There was a nice German family and a nice Japanese family, but they went to Manzanar. Judges came from our neighborhood. If you worked hard, you could make it to the top. No one had prejudice. I don't remember anyone treating us badly. Now, those illegals are ruining everything.

RICK: Illegals?

ED: He's recording. Be careful.

SOPHIE: I don't care. It's these illegals that are causing the problems. Illegals during Prop one eighty-seven. They were complaining, showing a Mexican flag on the news, saying they were going to take back California. It's their lousy government that's forcing them over here, and when they get here they apply for welfare. We didn't get any welfare.

RICK: Logan Heights is different.

SOPHIE: Sure, all these illegals. My family fought and died for this country. We did not complain. We went to war and died. Remember Louie Canado fought in Okinawa? He lost most of his friends. They come to this country to have babies so they can get welfare, these illegals. Illegal is illegal.

RICK: But how did Tata feel about illegals?

SOPHIE: Your grandfather hated them. Oh, did he hate them. He used to feel worse about the illegals than anyone.

RICK: Who was his best friend?

SOPHIE: Leandro.

RICK: And he liked Leandro, right?

SOPHIE: Sure, but what does this have to do with illegals?

RICK: Where was Leandro born?

SOPHIE: Mexico. What does this have to do with illegals, Geraldo Rivera?

RICK: Leandro came to this country legally?

SOPHIE: Uh, well, no. I don't know.

RICK: Then most likely, he was illegal. Right?

SOPHIE: Yes.

ED: He's going to go for the jugular.

RICK: Then he was an illegal. Then Leandro should have been turned in by Tata since he hated illegals so much.

SOPHIE: He was a good illegal. He worked. He put his son through college as a gardener. He wouldn't take social security.

RICK: Why?

SOPHIE: Because he did not want to spit on the Mexican flag and tear it up.

MARY: Oh, yeah.

SOPHIE: He thought he would have to spit on the Mexican flag to get social security.

RICK: I thought you just filled out forms.

SOPHIE: Oh, that's what he believed. But he was a good illegal. *(Beat.)* Well, we better get going.

RICK: Well, I hope you're not leaving because of me.

SOPHIE: No.

ED: Are you going to write about Sophie?

RICK: No, but if I did, you would come out looking really good.

SOPHIE: Okay, good. Well, we better get going. Come on, Marlo. *(As she leaves, she turns around calmly.)* When Marlo was out of work for all that time, people would say, "Tell him to get welfare," and I said, "You know I can't do that." But those illegals sure are getting welfare. Good-bye.

RICK: Is she leaving to go to one of those light-up-the-border meetings?

ED: Leave her alone. She worked hard her whole life. She's got a right to complain

MARLO: *(Runs back in.)* Hey, Rick, if you ever need anyone to do stunts in your films, I'm available. I can get hit in the head or the stomach and it won't bother me. I just wanted to tell you that. *(Runs back outside.)*

RICK: Dad, what went wrong?

MARY: *(Walks over to the TV room.)* I want to watch the news. The police shot a dog they had got complaints about.

(Ed gets up, then falters.)

MARY: Eddie, why don't you nap and forget about these memories? It's not good to keep living in the past.

ED: I think I should tell a little bit more.

RICK: What was it like during the war?

ED: Which one? Vietnam or World War II?

RICK: World War II.

ED: That was a good one. I was seventeen. *(The stage grows darker as down stage we hear the Movie Tone news music. Then we see the slide projector: "1943 Tuna Cannery in San Diego, California." We hear Edward R. Morrow's voice announcing.)*

ANNOUNCER: American workers fighting the imperial army at home, not with bullets but with sweat. United together helping this great nation in her time of need. All except for a lone Mexican woman in a cannery in San Diego.

(Lights reveal Josefina Najera, the same woman who portrays Mary Najera, grabbing a microphone while pushing a man aside.)

JOSEFINA/MARY: You can't kick me out. I came to this union meeting to tell you all that there's a better union for the workers and they have a right to know about it. Listen to me, the other union will give us health benefits and better wages. You don't have to settle for less. As for me, I am going to sign people up for it. You can't kick me out of this union. You crooked *pendejos*. I paid my dues. I'm a member of this union.

UNION OFFICER: Well, we don't accept your dues, m'am. So as far as we're concerned, you haven't paid any dues. Therefore, you do not belong to our union.

JOSEFINA: *(Throws out some money.)* There you go. Those are my dues.

UNION OFFICER: M'am, take your money. We can't accept it.

JOSEFINA: You're a *pendejo* and a liar.

UNION OFFICER: What does *pendejo* mean? No speaking Spanish here. This is San Diego, California, not Mexico, young lady. This is America.

JOSEFINA: If I wanted to be in Mexico, I would be there. And if I want a better union, I'll help start one.

UNION OFFICER: Are you a Communist? M'am, I am warning you, you will be blacklisted.

JOSEFINA: From a tuna cannery? I'll put you *en la lista negra. Ya te voy a echar el mal de ojo.* I am no Communist, *ni una comunista.* I got a son overseas. I got a star in the window. What do you have?

UNION OFFICER: Would someone please escort the Spanish woman outside.

JOSEFINA: Don't call me Spanish. That's just a Mexican with a few thousand in the bank. I'm going to leave, but I know where your car is.

CHON/ED: *(Chon, played by Ed, walks on stage and grabs Josefina. He is passionate and wild.)* Come on, baby. (SOTTO VOCCE IN SPANISH.) *¿Quieres que te meta un golpe?*

JOSEFINA: *Ahorita hablamos. (To the union officer.) Usted va a oir de mi abogado. Esto es un delito, un crimen.*

UNION OFFICER: They're talking in Spanish again. Can someone stop them from speaking Spanish? *(Chron makes a punching motion.)* Oh, geez, that does not look good.

ANNOUNCER: Tempers fly and fish smell in the San Diego Cannery as the one lone blacklisted, possibly Communistic,

Mexican woman battles the union. *(Black and white slides of people of that era—Stalin Tojo—flash as the announcer reads his movie reel copy. Cron and Josefina walk off stage. They kiss passionately.)*

JOSEFINA/MARY: Chon, I don't want you to hurt that man, no matter how badly he insulted me. Unless you see him at a bar with his fat fingers trying to paw some waitress.

CHON/ED: He ever touch you? I know how beautiful you are, how men want you.

JOSEFINA: It's not me. It's men. *(She seductively brushes her hair.)* I'm innocent. Remember when we were young, how you got me?

CHON: *(Takes out some candy kisses and gives them to her.)* Sure, I threw these in front of you and you followed the trail into my arms.

JOSEFINA: I gave myself away so young. You shouldn't have trusted me then. I gave myself away so cheaply. Men have always hurt me. Poor me. I think of that cruel man getting out of the union meeting around ten and getting in his 1941 blue Cadillac, license plate number F345U76, and my blood just boils. *(She starts to kiss Chon.)* Your hands are so strong.

CHON: From kneading the bread in the bakery.

JOSEFINA: No one scares you, Chon.

CHON: You do. *(They kiss.)* What was that license plate number?

JOSEFINA: I wrote it on a piece of paper by the bed. I knew it would come in handy someday.

CHON: What time did you say the meeting was finished?

JOSEFINA: Oh, Chon, I wrote it down for you. Now shut up. Let's go in the bedroom. I know what you're planning.

CHON: Am I?

JOSEFINA: Don't act stupid. If you're gonna do it, plan it so you don't get caught. Now, let's go into the bedroom. *(Black out.)*

ANNOUNCER: Americans fighting abroad and Americans peacefully getting along at home. Waiting for our boys to return.

ED: *(Lights up on old Ed sitting on a Lazy Boy with a hot water bottle against his throat.)* Your grandparents are very loving people.

RICK: Did she get her union?

ED: Yeah, she won.

RICK: How long were you overseas?

ED: Nearly three years. I came back skinny and sick. I was also nervous and irritable. I was suffering from delayed stress, but at that time there wasn't supposed to be any stress. I loved the Navy. I was born to be at sea. When I came home to San Diego, the world changed. There were two worlds: one before the war and one after.

RICK: Did you have a nice home coming?

ED: Oh, yeah, the Navy saw to that. *(We hear a crashing of a cell door as Ed is thrown in a jail. A sailor walks on stage. He is a black man and smoking a cigarette. The sailor comes up to Ed. Another white sailor is with him.)* It was nice to be home except for being arrested for desertion or AWOL. I wasn't on this ship. They arrested me for desertion. They were going to give me a dishonorable discharge. But I refused to plead guilty. I knew they were wrong. At that time, the Navy was hard. They gave a man ten years in Leavenworth because he jumped his ship in San Francisco to look after his kids when his wife died. *(Lights up on jail again, soundproof jail door clanging shut. A black man/actor #2 enters holding his file. He is manacled and followed by two Marines. He sits down and looks around. He says nothing. Next to him is a white man. They all hold their files. After a quick beat they pass their files around.)* Cigarette?

BLACK MAN: No, thanks.

ED: No. You got a cigarette?

BLACK MAN: I ain't even got a belt or shoelaces.

ED: Says here in your file that you're here for White Slavery.

BLACK MAN: My people tried the other kind before, but I got to tell you, White Slavery is much nicer.

WHITE MAN: Says you're in for desertion and refusing to obey orders and assault. *(White guy passes file to black man.)*

BLACK MAN: You assault the enemy, they give you a medal. Says here you ate light bulbs.

WHITE MAN: Anything to get me out of here.

BLACK MAN: They got two homosexuals. But they're in separate cells.

BLACK MAN: Them making us carry our files with us is a great idea. Keeps us honest.

ED: Helps to encourage reading. *(Reads.)* You are being court-martialed for disobeying and refusing to follow orders.

BLACK MAN: Here's your dental records and service records. Got bad teeth in the Pacific and wounded. I refused to go into a burning munitions ship.

ED: I heard about you guys. You wouldn't put out that fire on that burning ship.

BLACK MAN: It was a munitions boat, enough explosives to level a couple of blocks. The officer was white. He figured he'd risk black lives, not whites. Wouldn't send in white sailors. I'm no coward. That boat was about to blow. He was going to send us in to put the fire out. I saw it in his eyes. Wouldn't send in white sailors, just us. That's why I wouldn't do it.

ED: What?

BLACK MAN: You don't know nothing. You're Mexican.

ED: I'm American.

BLACK MAN: You always going to be Mexican to them. You ain't never gonna be just an American.

ED: I was during the war. I was an American. We all were.

BLACK MAN: He said, "I need some of you blacks to get in there." He wasn't sending in Americans to die. He was sending in blacks. That's when I said, enough is enough.

ED: They can't court-martial you for disobeying an order that would get you killed.

BLACK MAN: No, they can't, but they can for mutiny. They called us mutineers. Not obeying a white man is mutiny in this man's Navy. Don't expect better for you Mexican men.

ED: *(Reading.)* Twenty years?

BLACK MAN: I'm the only one who got sentenced. You been sentenced yet?

ED: No. I barely have been charged.

BLACK MAN: Well, you better act crazy to get out of this.

ED: I'm not crazy.

BLACK MAN: That's good, but you may spend ten years thinking about how sane you are in Leavenworth.

ED: I am feeling kinda disturbed. What would make me seem crazy?

WHITE MAN: I tried eating light bulbs.

BLACK MAN: After that truth-serum thing that boy was standing tall. See that guard down the hall. You got to knock him out. Act crazy. You know what I'm saying?

ED: Yeah, the little guard.

BLACK MAN: You want to be crazy, you got to get the other guy.

ED: The big guy?

BLACK MAN: Yeah, the one with mitts the size of hams. Anyone who would hit him has to be crazy.

ED: The little guy looks pretty tough. He's a scraper. Why not take him on?

BLACK MAN: Good luck, Mexican man. Hey, guards, come here! You better hit me.

ED: I can't hit you.

BLACK MAN: It's got to look real. *(Ed hits him.)* Goddamn! I told you to make it real, not kill me. *(He hits Ed, Ed hits him. A real fight breaks out.)*

ED: Come on, let's go.

BLACK MAN: Guards, help! This man's crazy. He's trying to kill me He's nuts. *(Breathless, he falls on the ground and says sotto vocce...)* Good luck! *(Jail doors open. Black out. A silhouette of a giant man is seen on the wall. Ed looks at the other sailors.)*

ED: You don't scare me, shortstop. Come at me. *(Black out. In the darkness we hear a shuffle and the punches of a man being pummeled. Lights up. We see Ed on the floor, bruised and beaten.)*

BLACK MAN: You did good, man. That was a great performance. You can get up now.

ED: No, I really can't.

BLACK MAN: Good. Make 'em think you're hurt.

ED: I'm hurt bad.

BLACK MAN: Good. Get sympathy and get 'em thinking you're crazy.

ED: Next time, I'm just going to do the ten years.

BLACK MAN: I would have eaten a light bulb. I would have passed a wicker chair before I took a beating like that. You even got me to believe you were crazy. I hear they're transferring you to medical. They're going to check you out.

BLACK MAN: Hey, Mexican man, don't forget me. I'll never get out of here. My black ass is going to rot in here. You can make it for me. Every day you're out of here, think of me. Don't forget me. *(Ed just lies there barely able to move. Two sailors come in and transfer him out.)* Don't forget me.

SOPHIE: *(Lights come up on another part of the stage. The scene opens up and we see a younger Sophie running into a room where Josefina is. They are in a hospital waiting room.)* They say he's crazy.

JOSEFINA: He's not crazy. Louie's crazy. Now shut up. They hurt my boy...

SOPHIE: I'll never get married. My father goes to jail for cockfighting. My mother is a former blacklisted cannery worker. And now Eddie's crazy. What next? Dad's in jail for cockfighting again. *(Ed enters under guard in a white medical uniform. Josefina and Sophie are across from Ed.)*

JOSEFINA: They're saying you're crazy. There saying you're a deserter.

ED: Sophie, I'm going to the newspapers. And I'm going to get back my paper route.

SOPHIE: Thank God he's crazy. I almost thought he said he was going to be in the newspapers. I'd just die.

JOSEFINA: Sophie, get out of here and let me talk to Eddie. *(Sophie leaves as Ed begins to speak.)*

ED: Loose lips sink ships, sailor. Don't feed 'em malarkey about me.

JOSEFINA: (In Spanish.) *¿Porqué dicen eso?*

ED: If I'm *not* crazy, I could spend ten years in jail.

JOSEFINA: Well, you do seem a little crazy, come to think of it. It's this damn country. It's crazy that you spent your time fighting for these people. This is how they pay you back: rules, procedures, anything to take something from us. It's not fair.

ED: Did you win your case?

JOSEFINA: I won my case. The cannery has to give me a year's back pay. But I won't take it. The union is to blame, not the cannery. I won't cash the check. It's the principle.

ED: Now *you're* crazy. Cash the check. They're going to give me sodium penethol. The doctors are going to see if I'm crazy for real. *(Sailor enters.)*

JOSEFINA: *(Loudly.)* What have you done to him? He doesn't recognize his own mother.

SAILOR: Time's up, Najera.

JOSEFINA: You know your father's rooster Felipe? He had something wrong with his throat, so one time Chon operated on him. Unfortunately, he died during the operation;

so whatever was wrong with his throat must have killed him.

ED: What?

JOSEFINA: Chon says never trust doctors. He says that Felipe, his rooster, did and look what happened to him. *(Lights fade as Ed steps into another area of the stage. Somberly he sits down on a chair. Then he talks plainly.)*

RICK: *(To audience.)* They were supposed to give him sodium penethol to see if he was really crazy. But this guy told him if he took lots of aspirin, it wouldn't be as effective and they wouldn't be able to get information from him. *(A man in a doctor's lab coat steps closer.)*

DOCTOR: What was the man's name?

ED: *(Groggily.)* Phil Johnson, the orderly on C block. Am I drugged? Is my aspirin idea working?

DOCTOR: Real well. You're telling us nothing. You're in an altered state.

ED: *(Laughs.)* What state am I in?

DOCTOR: You're in an altered state.

ED: I thought I was in California. *(Laughs.)* I am planning to escape and start a whore house in Mexico with Phil.

DOCTOR: The white slaver?

ED: Yes.

DOCTOR: How'd you get here?

ED: There was a sailor in charge of assignments. He wanted me shipped out. He didn't like me.

DOCTOR: The one you struck?

ED: Yes.

DOCTOR: Where was he shipping you?

ED: On a slow ship to Taiwan. I don't want to hear no more guns. I was about to finish my service and I wasn't going overseas any more. I was home. I'm home. I'm not cargo freight. I am a man. *(We see a panel of Army men seated facing upstage. A bugle sound is heard. We also see a sailor/actor 31 in a neck brace who walks in to testify.)*

OFFICER: This case is the United States Navy vs. Ed Najera. The purpose of this hearing is to determine if Lt. Ed Najera will get an honorable or dishonorable discharge. Sailor, proceed with your testimony.

SAILOR: Sir, I may not have gone overseas or served in any battles, but San Diego was no picnic either. He looked so smug. I know those people, they don't want to work. They're lazy. I assigned him on a departing ship to China, but he refused to take orders.

OFFICER: Wasn't his enlistment up in a month? He'd have to serve an extra six months because you thought he was smug?

SAILOR: Uh, he struck me, sir. He's a scrapper. His people love to fight. He got me with a sucker punch.

OFFICER: Where did he strike you?

SAILOR: On the chin.

OFFICER: When did he strike you?

SAILOR: He was going on the ship after the dentist visit.

OFFICER: What dentist visit?

SAILOR: He had to get some dental work. Three days worth, but I made them do it in four hours. They forgot to give him anesthesia, They had to do it so fast. Then he struck me again, at least five times, I believe. *(Ed is sitting in his chair. Doctor lights cigarette.)*

DOCTOR: Did you lose many friends in combat?

ED: Yeah, about five. One night they invited me to play guitar with them in their tent. I didn't go 'cause I wanted to see a Ginger Rogers' movie. A Zero crashed into their tent and they were all killed. Pops was killed. Pops was the oldest. We called him Pops 'cause he was so old. He was twenty-six. *(He rubs his shoulder.)*

DOCTOR: Why are you rubbing your shoulder?

ED: It's where I'm wounded.

DOCTOR: It's not in your report.

ED: Stupid report. During all the air raids, I lost two friends to those bombings.

DOCTOR: One last question. Are you crazy? Ed, are you crazy?

ED: No.

DOCTOR: *(Walks up to officers and reports.)* No, he is not crazy. We were. He had already served. He was a month away from an honorable discharge. We were about to ship him out again. We let bureaucracy nearly destroy a young man. I recommend an honorable discharge and all charges be dropped. He just wanted to come home. And that's real sane.

JUDGE: We are not in the habit of being lenient, but he should go home. God help us if we came back to bureaucratic, pencil-pushing bastards. Charges dismissed. *(Lights fade up. We see Rick with old Ed. He's giving him pills. The time is present. Ed is wrestling with Rick.)*

ED: That's morphine. I don't like to take too many.

RICK: The doctor wants you to take these. It'll help with the pain.

ED: *(Angrily.)* I want the pain. That way I'll feel it. You know when you don't feel a thing? Like being dead? Well I'm alive, I feel plenty, even pain. I count it a blessing to feel pain. I don't want the morphine. I'm still in charge.

RICK: You're stubborn, tarco.

ED: *Terco. God. It's terco, not tarco.* Tarco sounds like a fast food invention, I should have taught you Spanish.

RICK: Well, you had your chance.

ED: Stubborn. When you were about seven I bought you a varoom bike. Remember that? They made a varoom noise. You used to wake me up in the morning under my bedroom window going varroom, varoom, varoom, so loud. I'd tell you to knock it off, but you'd just stand there smiling varoom, varoom. You were *terco* then.

RICK: Then one day, someone stole the varoom box off the bikes and they were just bikes. They didn't make any noise. What happened?

ED: To your bikes? I don't know, but I bet Steve does. *(He tries to get up.)* I'm wounded but I'm not down yet. I'm resting. I'm not taking that medicine. Get me a shake. Where's Mary?

RICK: What happened in the war?

ED: Well, they put me under and found out I was telling the truth. Don't tell that story. How's the job search coming?

RICK: Oh, great. I might get a job working with some of the most highly paid miserable people in the world. I sometimes wish I could come home to San Diego.

ED: You can. But I don't think you should.

RICK: God, you're naive. Your optimism sometimes really hurts.

ED: "Argue your limitations and be sure enough they're yours." Read Dale Carnegie, Rick. It would be good for you.

RICK: *(Changing subject.)* So you got an honorable discharge?

ED: Oh, yeah, then I went civilian. It was great. But San Diego had changed. There were no jobs like during the war. This town is a war town. Korea hadn't happened yet, so I got a job with Louie Canado working at a rendering plant.

RICK: Did you ever encounter racism?

ED: No, I don't remember. Have you?

RICK: No.

ED: Me neither. We were Americans after the war, not Mexican Americans or Chicanos. We were just Americans. *(Louie Canado walks up to Ed. They take a sheet and put it in the air and shake it out. Grinding and machinery is heard in the background.)* I know this is a bad job, but it's the only one we can get. Louie, don't be a hothead.

LOUIE/ACTOR #2: Damn, Eddie, we could get better jobs in Mexico. Our parents never dreamed we would be doing this. We fought a war for the right to work at a rendering plant? This is nothing but a glue factory. They promised us ten dollars a day. They're only giving us eight. This job is shit. You're only a hero if you're an Anglo. *(A filthy fore-man walks up. He is Actor #1.)*

ED: You're making this sound worse than it is.

FOREMAN: All right, all of you workers, everyone, line up in rows. Welcome to the exciting world of rendering. Some of you are new here, some have been here a while. We are no longer called a glue factory. We are now a professional rendering plant, and I am your rendering-plant manager. I'm sure you would like one of those nice cushy jobs, but this is manual labor and you should do it well. Plus, half of your names are Manuel. *(Laughs.)* I would like your input and creativity, suggestions on how we could be more efficient. But not 'til I ask.

ED: Uh, sir, there's a discrepancy in our checks.

FOREMAN: Not now. You men are going to walk away from here with some memories. There is excitement here. I remember one time, the elephant from the zoo got stuck in the gears of the grinder. That was fun.

ED: But, sir, I should've been paid more.

FOREMAN: Not now. Now you got to listen to instructions. The first thing to do is to lift the cowhide, shake out the maggots and blood, put cowhide back on the other side and shake out the cowhide. I'm sure you will feel some discomfort from the salt entering your cut wounds on your hands, but after a few hours a day you'll barely notice. Old workers will be responsible for teaching all the newcomers.

ED: Right? See, once you say it, it isn't so bad. But, sir, we need to talk about this check.

FOREMAN: Other days you will lift sixteen tons of rotten tuna for rendering. That will be on lucky days. *(A grizzled worker comes in, the same actor who plays Cherie.)*

GRIZZLED WORKER: I'm a knife thrower. Stand against the wall. I'm going to be a knife thrower. I can do it. I'm going to be in the circus.

FOREMAN: Ralph, don't make me send you home early. Hey, where's my dog?

GRIZZLED WORKER: *(Looking guilty.)* He was standing next to the grinder just a moment ago, Dad. He was over there by the machinery. I'm sure he's around here somewhere. I'm going to find him. Here, Poochi... Here, Poochi...

FOREMAN: Goddamn it, get on home. All you people get to work. I catch any one of you being lazy and it's "Hit the street, don't skip a beat." And no talking Spanish.

EDDIE: Sir, about the check?

FOREMAN: Later. *(Foreman exists. They constantly work as they talk.)*

ED: Louie, we got jobs. You ever read Norman Vincent Peale? We need to work on our self-improvement. It is everything. Today, slinging guts to make fertilizer, so we can make roses grow pretty. Think of us as rose-makers, not two Joe's working and sweating at a rendering plant. We're rose-makers. I just like to get a fair wage.

LOUIE: We have been working here three months, but he always treats us like we started today. He forgets. He thinks we're one of the other Mexicans.

ED: "If you argue your limitations, they're yours." In Toastmasters, you learn public speaking. The world's our oyster, Louie. Pass me that rotten hide. *(Louie hands him another sheet.)* I've been reading this book about success, "How to Win Friends and Influence People." *(Foreman angrily enters. He walks up to Louie and Ed.)*

FOREMAN: A little less talking, more work, boys.

ED: Uh, Mr. Johnson, we've been working here three months and we don't get paid as much as you promised when we started. We negotiated a different salary than what appears on our checks.

FOREMAN: What do you need extra money for? You're just going to spend money on getting drunk and women and fighting. You ain't going to buy no property.

ED: What we choose to spend money on is our business and of no concern to you. On a set rate.

LOUIE: Damn, you've been going to Toastmasters.

FOREMAN: I didn't understand you, son.

ED: You're cheating us.

FOREMAN: Oh, you said the wrong thing, son. You might as well have called me a liar. I was division champion of the Navy in thirty-two. Oh, yeah, I'm kicking ass and taking names. I'm going to enjoy this. *(He takes off his coat.)*

ED: I was a champion in forty-two. *(Ed takes off his coat.)*

FOREMAN: Come on, you uppity Mexican trying to get higher wages. I'll beat you white. Now this fight is just between you and me, so don't go calling in your gang. I know how you all fight. Just me and you. You hotheaded non-American, come on, you're stealing jobs from deserving Americans and complaining. I'm going to beat the malarkey out of you. To think I gave you a chance so I could hear you complaining and calling me a liar. *(Ed knocks him out with one punch.)*

LOUIE: Is this winning friends and influencing people? You sure did influence him. But I don't think he'll want to be your friend.

ED: I hear enough speeches in Toastmasters. I think I influenced us out of a job. Well, Louie, I guess were unemployed. *(Big band music switches to early forties boogie-woogie, then to early rock and roll. Flashes of San Diego fill the back screen. Nineteen forty-six. Ed walks over to Mary, a young girl at a bus stop.)*

LOUIE: Who's that girl?

ED: I don't know. But I'm going to marry her.

LOUIE: Damn, Buddy, you look good in your outfit. You look like Dillinger.

ED: I got a silver whisky flask. *(Mary stands.)*

MARY: *(To herself.)* Oh Lord, a pachuco. Why's he staring at me?

ED: Excuse me, I could not help but notice you. Where are you from?

MARY: I'm an Indian princess from a reservation.

ED: I normally don't butt in where I'm not wanted.

MARY: Well, you're right. You're not wanted.

ED: Listen, Indian princess, you got to be careful in a big city. There's lots of strange guys. You can only trust guys like me. That's the first rule.

MARY: All I need to know is what the nuns taught me.

ED: What did they teach you?

MARY: If you sit on a boy's lap you have to have a telephone book between you and him.

ED: And they're right.

MARY: I got to go. *(She starts to leave.)*

ED: Where are you going, princess? Back to the reservation to collect some more scalps?

LOUIE: Smooth.

MARY: Scalps? Oh, you sure have an imagination. I don't have time to scalp *pachucos* right now, 'cause I'm going to a dance.

LOUIE: *(Pointing to Ed.)* Well, this *pachuco* can jitterbug like no one can. (Louie laughs.)

MARY: I would like to see that. But this is a chaperoned dance at the Coffee Club in Balboa Park. It starts around eight. It's open to the public. Plus, there's a dress code. So I'm sure I won't be seeing you there. My name's Mary, but don't tell anyone you're my guest. Don't ask for me.

ED: Hear that, Louie? Mary, like the Virgin Mary.

LOUIE: Good, Ed, you go after the virgin. I'm going to look up that redhead in Tijuana.

ED: I'm going to get that girl, Louie. You watch. I'm going to marry her. *(Lights change. 1947 music plays fast and sensual. Ed and Mary are now at the dance. He reaches his hand out and grabs her. They start to dance to the music. Slides of San Diego swirl past them. It shows the passage of time as we see a five-month courtship happening in five* *minutes, all the while that they are dancing, music ranges from juke box "Kiss me once and kiss me once again" to latin music of the forties. The dialogue that follows happens as if it were part of a song and dance number.)*

MARY: I can't believe you're here.

ED: Lots of squares here...

MARY: They're good kids from good families, doctors' kids. Don't you have a girlfriend?

ED: No, and I'm not looking for one. So don't get your hopes up. You're a kid. I don't need to be looking after anyone.

MARY: *(He lifts her up as part of a dance move. Very Fred Astaire-like.)* What does your father do?

ED: He's a baker.

MARY: It's proper if I meet your family. Especially since we're going steady. *(Ed twirls her in a dance move and moves away.)*

ED: We're going steady? I don't want to get serious. I got plans. I'm going to be a photographer, join Toastmasters. Be a top salesman on the pots and pans circuit.

MARY: Then, why did you ask me to marry you?

ED: I didn't ask you to marry me. I thought it, but hold on now. You're leading this dance. *(They twirl with Mary leading.)*

MARY: Well, okay, I'll marry you, but I have to meet your parents.

ED: *(Confused.)* Mom, Dad, I want you to meet Mary. I think we're getting married.

CHON: (VOICE OVER.) Well, whatever you think is best. We're tired. Your mother and I have to go to bed.

ED: My parents are very enthusiastic people, very affectionate.

JOSEFINA: (VOICE OVER.) Where have you been?

ED: We went to Reno and got married.

CHON: (VOICE OVER.) Oh good. Let's go to bed, Josephina, it's late.

MARY: They sure do need to sleep a lot.

MARY: Uh, that went well.

ED: See, I didn't plan on getting married, saddled with a wife. I got plans. Do you think I'm moving too fast?

MARY: Well, you know what's best. Besides, it's done. You're going to like marriage, really. The extra responsibility will be good for you. *(They twirl like a waltz.)*

ED: What responsibility?

MARY: Kids. We're going to have a baby. *(They stop dancing.)*

ED: I feel dizzy.

BLACK OUT.

(We are back in the present time. Ed is sitting in his chair reading a paper. On the radio we hear "This is Talk Radio 6.40, the John and Ken show. The question is, how do you feel about 911 operators being required to learn Spanish?")

ED: I feel dizzy. I feel cold. Can you bring me a blanket?

MARY: I did.

ED: Why is it cold in here? I'll have to do everything. Let me get it. I know what the right station is.

SOPHIE: (VOICE OVER.) Hello. Am I on the air? Well, if you ask me, if there is a fire and you were living in France, you better tell 'em about it in French. Those frog-eating bastards sure won't help you if you don't talk French. Well, I say if some illegals are choking on some menudo after plowing their uninsured car into some poor taxpayer while he was looking for the unemployment department so he could make some money, well, I say, let 'em choke. Let 'em scream in Spanish all they want. It's the illegals. Illegal is illegal.

ED: Rick, you be nice to Sophie, look after her. *(Lights reveal Mary walking toward Rick with a portable phone. Excited.)*

MARY: It's your agent.

RICK: Andy. *(On another part of the stage Andy appears. They both talk with their backs to each other.)*

ANDY: Hey, how you doing? Uh, listen I got some news for you. They made an offer.

RICK: Who? Great, what is it?

ANDY: It's not a good offer, but it's an offer. There's a show they don't need your voice around the table, but I got them to give you a chance. On a two-week trial period, for free. See, if they don't like you they don't have to pay you. In other words, it's a no-risk deal. It's a win-win situation with them winning a lot more than you.

RICK: Hitler gave Poland a better offer. Well, if they like me, they bring me on as a full writer?

ANDY: Well, they got this new ethnic program where they can hire you for half the salary for a total of thirteen weeks.

RICK: Half salary, what are you saying? I'm going to make half the salary of another writer and be in some program?

ANDY: You're great. You'll prove yourself within thirteen weeks and then they'll make you a regular writer with...

RICK: White writer's salary?

ANDY: Rick, why do you have to go there? Think about it, Okay?

RICK: Sure, Thanks. *(Hangs up the phone.)*

RICK: Fuck. Damn. Damn it. Oh God, what's with these people? *(He punches his fist on the floor, shattering his cellular phone.)*

MARY: Is something wrong?

RICK: No. Just this battery, a bad connection. *(Ed stumbles and falls. He struggles to get up. Rick goes to help him up.)*

ED: That damn rug. I slipped on it. Why would your mother put a dangerous rug there?

MARY: How did you do that?

ED: I guess I didn't lift my feet. You should get a shorter rug.

MARY: *(Going to get medicine.)* I'm going to get you your medicine. Rick, what did your agent have to say? Is anything wrong?

RICK: He said everything is great. *(Ed sits in his chair, winded.)* How you doing, Dad?

ED: Great, just great.

RICK: Yeah, just like me.

MARY: See, everything is great just the way I imagined it would be. Everything's great. *(Lights rise on the living room. Rick is looking at his father, who is asleep in a chair. A slide projector flashes images of family photos on the wall.)*

RICK: History is a funny thing. Memories are so fragile. I believe history is only history if it's alive. It's like worlds end. They slip by us. We see them going by us but it doesn't seem real. Films are more real to some people than actual history. People even doubt written history. Some people doubt that the Holocaust ever took place. History does not seem real. It's only real if it's repeated to us by it's survivors. What's my earliest memory? My grandfather used to put fighting roosters in front of me. And he was watching me trying to find a connection between our generations. Between us was a tornado of feathers, blood and mystery. He watched me to see what I was thinking. Maybe he wanted us to share some primordial rite together. What was he looking for in my eyes? I didn't speak Spanish and he didn't speak much at all. *(Steve, Rick's brother, walks in and quietly walks by Ed.)*

RICK: Steve, what are you doing here?

STEVE: I got a job interview.

RICK: I'd like to interview you.

STEVE: I could tell you things. But...

RICK: I know you could tell me things. But you would have to kill me afterwards.

STEVE: There would be no need for that. I could tell you things but I don't have time. I would tell you that you would not be classified. I don't trust you. *(Rick pushes the vase towards him like it's a mike.)*

RICK: You can trust me.

STEVE: I already checked the vase. It's clean.

RICK: Steve, are there UFO's? Can you tell me that at least? Are there UFO's?

STEVE: Yes, good-bye.

RICK: My brother worked for the government. He has me so paranoid. I can't say what he did, nor do I really know. Once I wrote some things about him, but my computer went down. Who knows? They could be watching us all right now. I last knew my brother during Vietnam. I remember that's the last time I really saw him. He took me to see John Wayne in the *Green Berets,* which formed our views on the war. That movie turned me into a Republican; Wilson turned me into a Democrat. Oh, yeah, he's a great presidential candidate. He hired an illegal alien. "Uh, María, make the bed, then I'll deport you." Vietnam hurt my family, make no mistake. *(Sixties music plays; Jimmy Hendrix's "All Along the Watch Tower." A sleeping Ed is in the Lazy Boy Chair. Cherie, Rick's sister (played by Sophie), and Steve enter. Steve is in uniform, Cherie is in Woodstock apparel.)*

CHERIE: See, I get a bad feeling about this. The vibe is wrong. The government doesn't care about us, man. We are just like the wildebeest's herd. That's what we are. We are grazing peacefully waiting for the lion to strike. When he attacks, we run. That's all we can do, and hope we are not devoured by the lion in the night. So we stick close to the herd and hope the lion kills our neighbor, our friend, the weaker one, but not us, never us. We pray to God for luck, but eventually we all must fall. Eventually our name is "the other one." I'm boycotting Vietnam. I suggest you do it, too, and get in touch with your feminine side.

STEVE: Geez, you depress the hell out of me. You are just too damn educated to understand this war. Sure, we run with the herd and we're damn glad. We count the dead instead of getting counted. See, when I read the *National Geographic,* I look for pictures of the native girls. I want to be the lion for once. We should attack, not retreat. We got to have the guts to run the world or someone else will and it sure ain't gonna be a woman.

CHERIE: How much of the world do you own?

STEVE: Always gotta have the last word. Okay, this is how it works. Rick will represent South Vietnam and Clint will represent North Vietnam. Rick, if you kick Clint's ass, I'll give you a gallon of ice cream and five dollars.

CHERIE: All right, I don't have as much as Steve, but Clint, I know you're scrappy. Tell you what, for one dollar, a package of Cheetos and a ride on my motorcycle, I want you to kick Rick's bourgeois spoiled ass. Also the hallway is your demilitarized zone. *(They both look over the lip of the stage as we hear arguing and fighting.)*

CHERIE: North Vietnam is kicking South Vietnam's ass.

STEVE: I guess I'm no longer going to be an advisor. I better go in and help.

CHERIE: You're escalating.

STEVE: *(Rick walks up to his father. Before he does, he turns to the audience.)* Shut up, hippie.

RICK: *(To the audience.)* To this day, my little brother and I don't get along. War wounds don't heal easily.

ED: *(Wakes up.)* I was just sleeping. I've been doing that more often. Let's record 'em some more. I'm beginning to like this. If I start not to talk, it means my throat hurts. I'll give you a signal.

RICK: What kind of signal?

ED: I'll throw a shoe at you.

RICK: Let's talk about Vietnam.

ED: See *Platoon?*

RICK: Did you ever go on a patrol?

ED: No, I didn't, but one of the guys that was sent from North Island did. He actually went out on a patrol with some Marines.

RICK: What happened to him?

ED: Nothing. But he killed himself after he got back to San Diego. Vietnam was hot and spooky and my job was just to fix the jet's helicopters. War's about making money for somebody. Basically, we went over there to protect our interest. If it's not valuable, we won't be there. I was there for the overtime. A lot of companies were there. From Coca-Cola to Exxon. We were defending the Vietnamese's right to choose between Pepsi or Coca-Cola.

STEVE: *(Comes back in.)* What is he asking now?

ED: About Vietnam.

STEVE: I don't want to talk about it. John was in Morocco avoiding the draft while I was serving. I was around there. That's all I can say. You were too young to remember. I think I may have this job.

RICK: Great, Steve, I'm happy for you. Hey, I almost saw you smile.

ED: See, for every "no" you get, you're getting closer to that "yes." *(Steve exits. Lights change and we hear the song "Sitting on the Dock of the Bay." We see Rick and Ed fishing. Ed pulls out a line hook with bait and a mobile of artificial fish.)*

DICK: *(Holding a lure.)* Dad, how does this lure work?

ED: I made it at the base, Rick. It is based on fish psychology. All these artificial little fish around the bait are there to simulate a bunch of fish trying to take the bait. It looks like a school of greedy little fish are going after the bait. Now, a real fish sees it and it stimulates their greed response because fish have very low self-esteem. That's why they're always in large schools. This overrides his caution response and he doesn't worry about the hook. He takes the bait and is captured.

RICK: Wow, you made this at the Navy base? You must have a lot of free time on your hands.

ED: Yeah, I'm a government worker. We all do. The government's good to us, Rick. They give us these pens as a bonus. See how they say property of U.S. Government? It is a patriotic pen, son. *(Ed pulls out a ballpoint pen. Back* *in present time. Ed walks slowly over to his chair. Rick is holding a pen.)*

RICK: *(To Ed.)* You still got these pens?

ED: They're made to last, Rick.

RICK: I always felt paranoid using these pens. I thought someone was gonna come and say, "Hey you're not the U.S. Government. Where did you get this pen?" *(Ed reaches for one of his shakes. He looks at the TV. In the background we hear AMC classics, the music theme.)*

ANNOUNCER: Next week on AMC we feature a Burt Lancaster Festival starting with *TELL 'EM VALDEZ IS COMING*, a movie Burt Lancaster did late in his career, where he plays an old Mexican Federale seeking revenge.

ED: I loved that movie. I'm gonna stay alive till next week! *(He picks up the remote control and lowers the volume. The TV Ed watches is now facing the audience. Over the stage a panel of a few old black and white TV's are on.)* I used to love to go to the movies with you.

RICK: That's how I got interested in the arts. You took me to see a British film and you loved how they talked. I wanted to make you proud.

ED: Yeah, I said if you could talk as beautiful, I would be so proud of you. Do some Shakespeare.

RICK: It's been a while.

ED: Do it for me.

RICK: I don't want to.

ED: My dad, at fifty, could ask me to wash his car and I would. That's the kind of respect I have for my dad. *(On the television monitors, we see a movie clip of Laurence Olivier in Henry V Act 3 Scene 1. Simultaneously, we see Rick doing the same speech as Laurence Olivier.)*

RICK: "Once more unto the breach,
dear friends, once more,
Or close the wall up with our English dead.
In peace there's nothing so becomes a man
As modest stillness, and humility,

But when the blast of war blows in our ears,
Then imitate the action of the tiger.
Stiffen the sinews, conjure up the blood,
Disguise fair nature with hard-favoured rage.
Then lend the eye a terrible aspect.
Let it pry through the portage of the head
Like the brass cannon, let the brow o'erwhelm it
As fearfully as doth a galled rock
O'erhang and jutty his confounded base,
Swilled with the wild and wasteful ocean.
Now set the teeth and stretch the nostril wide, hold hard
the breath, and bend up every spirit to his full height!
On, on, you noblest English,
Whose blood is fet from fathers of war-proof,
Dishounour not your mothers; now attest
That those whom you called fathers did beget you.
Be copy now to men of grosser blood,
And teach them how to war...
For there is none of you so mean and base
That hath not noble lustre in your eyes.
I see you stand like greyhounds in the slips,
Straining upon the start. The game's afoot.
Follow your spirit, and upon this charge
Cry, 'God for Harry, England
and Saint George! *(Tries to change subject.)*
I wrote you a monologue. Here.

ED: *(Looks at it and starts to read it. He starts to get emotional.)* No one ever wrote me a monologue before. People think I'm brave, Rick, but I'm scared. *(Beat.)* You got to go outside. *(Rick exits. Old Ed picks up the tape recorder. Composes himself.)* I took the varoom box off your bike. I'm sorry, but damn it, you really could get up early. Yeah, you've made me proud. Selling door-to-door taught me my biggest lessons. You need to learn lessons to go on. Toastmasters taught me how to talk. Now my throat doesn't allow me to talk. Ironic, isn't it? See, in those days, people believed if you could speak well, you could do anything. And all I wanted to do was to speak well. *(Louie walks in. Ed is back in time.)*

LOUIE: What are we doing here, Eddie?

ED: Learning to talk. See, in Toastmasters, you can learn to talk. If you want to be a salesman, you got to learn to talk.

MAN: *(Walks to the middle of the stage.)* My name is Harry Stevenson. I work at North Island in shipping and I'm Vice President of this Toastmasters Club. Now I would like to do some oral interpretation of this piece.

LOUIE: Aw, man, let's get out of here before he tries to oral interpretate on us.

ED: Can you imagine, Louie, being able to talk to men and inspire them with words?

LOUIE: Can we make some money from this?

ED: You don't have the soul of a poet. We can use this. *(Ed walks up to an imaginary person with a suitcase.)*

ED: Hello, sir, can I have a moment? *(He hears a slam. Ed moves each time. He moves in a circle doing various moments of his speech.)* Yes, I have *(Slam.)* the best pots and pans and kitchen utensils *(Slam.)* that money can buy. *(Slam.)* These utensils will save you time. *(Slam.)* *(Ed starts to look dejected, then stands alone on the stage. The lights silhouette him.)*

> FRIENDS, SAN DIEGANS, COUNTRYMEN,
> lend me your ears;
> I come to bury the competition, not to praise it;
> the evil that men do lives after them.
> The shoddy work should be interred with their bones;
> so let it be with Tupperware.
> These noble pots and pans are made in America!
> Here, under leave of the Better Business Bureau and
> the rest,
> *(For Tupperware is an honorable product;*
> *So are they all; all honorable products.)*

Come I to speak America's funeral...
These are my products, faithful and just to me.
(He holds pots and pans.)
I speak not to disprove other products,
But here I am to speak what I do know.
You all did love Teflon once, not without cause:
What cause withholds you then to buy and order now.
Oh judgment! Thou art fled to brutish beasts,
And men have lost their reason... bear with me;
My heart is in the coffin with my sales.
And I must pause till it comes back to me.
(Applause is heard.)
Louie, I'm the top salesman in my region. Every "no"
I get, I know that I'm getting closer to that one "yes."
(Ed starts to slowly fall to the floor. It's almost a balletic falling in a circle. He falls to the floor. Rick walks in and sees his father lying on the floor.)

RICK: Dad, you okay?

ED: Yes. I just thought I would lie down awhile. I just need to lie dow

MARY: Eddie, you've got to lie down. Just let him lie down.

ED: I just need help into my room. That damn morphine makes me groggy. That's all. Don't count me out yet.
(Mary walks Eddie into his room, then returns.)

RICK: Why didn't you tell me he was this sick?

MARY: He didn't want to worry you.

RICK: How long has this been going on?

MARY: A long time. He doesn't want you to worry, so instead he has me worrying.

RICK: Why didn't you tell me something was wrong? I would've come down more often. I would've helped out more.

MARY: I'll be fine. The doctor gave me Prozac.

RICK: You're on Prozac?

MARY: I'm depressed. Your father's dying. There's no one to turn to. The government doesn't help. They don't even

know what he has. The government can't even employ
Steve anymore. Who's going to look after him? Huh?
Who's going to look after me? He is sick. Where have you
been? He's staying in his room more often, looking at pictures, talking to himself, watching that damn History
Channel and Court TV. He refuses to exercise. It's like
he's given up. I need help and I hate asking for it.

RICK: I could be here.

MARY: Oh, sure, you'll all be here. Well, taking care of an old
man isn't exciting. It's not glamorous. In this story you
keep interviewing him only. He's interesting 'cause he
went to war. What about raising five kids and looking
after your father now? Men glorify war 'cause it's easy to
know if you win or lose, have defeat or victory. Not with
children, not with people. This isn't glorious. They give no
one a medal for commitment nowadays. So I take Prozac.
So what? I'm a modern suffering mother, damn it. *(Beat.)*
I doubt if you'll even notice me. Well, I'm hurting, Rick. I
need help.

RICK: I'm sorry. I know who you are and I know what you've
done. I'm sorry if I ever made you feel slighted. I'm sorry.

MARY: No, I was being selfish. *(Laughs.)* Now you're not
going to write about me.

RICK: Sure, I will. I'll name the play after you. Mom, you're
named after Mary. You don't have to be her. One time I
was hurt.

MARY: When you got run over?

RICK: Yeah, I nearly died. I was crippled for a year.

MARY: I remember you couldn't walk.

RICK: You were over my body crying. They thought I might
die. Dad was off working, but you were with me. Crying,
you were crying over my body. I never saw you cry before.
You never told me you loved me, you showed it; but I'll
never forget that I looked at you and I never knew what
pure love was till that moment. I knew you loved me. I
could feel your tears on me. I wanted to live for you, so

much. I felt your love, I swear it kept me alive. Growing up, you weren't affectionate. You never said you loved me.

MARY: I had so little time. I worked three jobs.

RICK: You should have started and stopped with me.

MARY: You all wanted to be *only children*.

RICK: I would see all these other mothers at home with their kids.

MARY: That was the problem living in good neighborhoods on a bad neighborhood's salary. You only feel poor when you're surrounded by rich people.

RICK: But, Mom, I never felt unloved. I want you to know that, although I might fawn over Dad.

MARY: Oh well, you should fawn over your dad. He is sick and the attention's good for him. That's what I get, having so many sons. Boys need lots of attention and your dad, boy does he need attention. That's the secret to handling men. Give them lots of attention. I bet your dad's sleeping. Rick, why don't you get some rest?

RICK: I'm not tired, Mom. We used to have a garden in the back. We used to have all those fruit trees.

MARY: Oh, yes, he wanted to cement the back yard. He thought all those fruit trees were just too much trouble. He wanted the city in La Mesa. There used to be horses across the street.

RICK: There's a little sunlight left. I'm gonna go outside and work on the garden. I always wanted to build you a garden. I could fix up the back yard. We could plant a few trees.

MARY: Yeah, planting is good for the soul, makes you feel close to God. Stop and think: you know what Adam's job was in Eden?

RICK: I don't know.

MARY: Tending the garden. That's all he had to do, look after a garden. When he left the garden, everything went to hell. The nuns taught me that. Those nuns knew everything.

RICK: If he had a lawn blower, he might be Mexican.

MARY: I believe he was. *(Phone rings. Rick looks at the phone, goes to answer it, then decides against it.)*

MARY: What if it's your agent?

RICK: What if it is? I'm going to work outside in the garden. There's only a few hours of sunlight left. I can mow the lawn. Maybe work up a sweat. Then, I'm going to write down a story. *(Phone rings.)*

MARY: That's a good idea. I'm going to check on Eddie. *(Lights fade and Ed is looking at a photo of Chon Tata, Rick's grandfather. It's projected on the wall behind them.)*

ED: How you doing, Dad? You had a stroke. Make a fist, like you're going to teach me to box. Come on, would you? I know you miss her. Remember when she was in the hospital, you would say, "I love you," and she would say, "Now go to sleep." When she was in the hospital, I would say that and she would say, "I know, go to sleep. Rick's fine." I saw Rick in a play as a woman. But he played it real unconvincingly. I've been reading these poems by Gutiérrez Najera. You know, I was a poet. *(Ed looks at the book and reads a poem. Rick is on the other side of the stage, simultaneously speaking the words of the poem.)*

>   A MI PADRE,
>   Padre, en las recias luchas de la vida,
>   cuando mi pobre voluntad flaquea,
>   ¿quien, si no tú, me alienta la caída?
>   ¿Quien, si no tú, me ayuda en la pelea?

RICK:

>   FOR MY FATHER,
>   Father, in the strong fights of life,
>   when my own will weakens,
>   who but you, encourages me when I've fallen?
>   Who but you, aids me in my struggle? *(Fade Out.)*

(Rick walks in to his father's room. He's dirty from gardening.)

ED: What were you doing? You're dirty.

RICK: I was gardening. I mowed the lawn. I like the fields.

ED: We worked so hard to keep you out of the fields. Oh, soon as I get well, I plan to work around the house more. The fields?

RICK: It's okay. It was gardening, not picking. *(Rick decides to do his stand up. He picks up a ketchup bottle as a microphone and speaks. We hear the John Mendoza introduction from Rick's A&E Special.)* This is a command performance for the homebound. Hi, my name is Rick. I'm Mexican American. I was never in a street gang. I tried real hard, but I failed the written test. I'm light-skinned, my sister's dark. I have a lot of Spanish blood, but my sister's got all the Indian blood. I know that because when we were young, I stole her gold and made her build me beautiful Spanish missions in my back yard.

ED: Cherie's going to hate that joke.

RICK: Uh, oh, a heckler. Security, please. I've been in therapy to be less macho. I'm learning to say things like, "You make me sad when you act so stupid." Don't get me wrong. I don't come from a dysfunctional family, but like all Latinos, I would like to create one someday.

ED: Rick, I'm tired. I'm going to give you the signal, but I can't reach my shoe.

RICK: Sure, you rest. Good night, Dad. *(Rick exits. He walks to Mary, who is looking at the slide projector. Mary is looking at a family album; photos flash on the wall. You see the history of the family.)*

MARY: There's Eddie in Vietnam. There's you at the Globe. My brother, here in New Mexico, and here's you in a play, that television pilot.

RICK: Yeah, don't I look natural? You know what the studio told me? They wanted A. Martínez for my role or Jimmy Smitts. The studio had more reasons how to say no: "We don't like the lead." "We don't like the writing." "We have something similar." "We just don't like you." *(Steve enters.)* How's the job search?

STEVE: Fine. I just don't want to go overseas anymore. I spent so many years in the government, outside the government will be nice. *(He exits.)*

MARY: That is so good. He really opened up. He is learning to talk. That's a big step for him. Don't tease him.

RICK: Course not. *(Steve re-enters.)*

STEVE: Tell me, Rick, are you going to talk about yourself in the show?

RICK: No, not really. But I'm hoping if it ever goes on stage, Jimmy Smitts will play me.

STEVE: Your life's interesting, almost getting "La Bamba" and "The Desi Story." If Freddy Fender dies, you may play him.

RICK: Wow, he really is talkative. How do I get him to shut up?

STEVE: What's your one regret? Almost being a star?

RICK: No, almost having a marriage. *(Beat.)* Angela's my only regret.

STEVE: I guess that will be another play. Won't it?

MARY: Why can't you kids get along?

RICK: It's in our genes. We all are conquistadors at heart. I'm going outside to write.

STEVE: I was kidding.

MARY: *(Angrily.)* You don't know how to kid right. Why can't any of you say one thing nice? *(Rick is talking on a beat-up duct-taped cellular phone. He is talking to Andy.)*

ANDY: What's with your phone? It's a really bad connection. Well, anyway, they want an answer on their offer.

RICK: Is the offer going away if I don't answer them?

ANDY: No, but you should give them an answer soon. I know you don't need it. You can always work in Spanish-speaking television.

RICK: Sure, as long as my characters are mutes or Mexicans that ask where the library is.

ANDY: You lost me. I don't get it.

RICK: Welcome to another episode of *¿Donde está la biblioteca?* Andy, I really do speak bad Spanish. I'm an American. I want to write American shows.

ANDY: Give them an answer.

RICK: I'll give them an answer.

ANDY: What?

RICK: No. No. I have to decline.

ANDY: I know it's not much.

RICK: *(Angrily.)* I don't need much, just something to give him. I'm a modern wetback, Andy. I don't send my family money, I send them back fame. I need a show, a job, something to make my father proud. He's dying, Andy, dying. Do you understand? He's getting fucking canceled, but in real life. Now do you understand? Find me something to give him. Not a half-assed offer to be a house Mexican on some show. A real writing job.

ANDY: Wow, that's a lotta pressure, Rick. I got a call on line two. I've got to take this call. Think about it, okay? *(He hangs up the phone. His father walks in carrying a trench coat.)*

ED: That's called a hard sale.

RICK: You should be in bed.

ED: I couldn't sleep. I was worried that you were going to forget this coat. I want you to have it.

RICK: Thanks. I don't need it.

ED: Rick, doesn't it get cold in L.A.? I'm not using this coat; you should have it. Take it.

RICK: The last time you gave me a coat like this, I was in kindergarten. And I was so proud of it that I took it to school.

ED: You looked like little John F. Kennedy at his father's funeral. Then, at the end of the day, I saw you dragging it behind you. I remember saying, "What's wrong?"

RICK: I remember Nicky Whitt saying to me, "Where'd you get the dress?" I guess he must have been jealous or something.

ED: *(Laughs.)* You never wore that coat again. Remember
how some people at school called him Nit Whit?

RICK: Yeah, teachers can be so cruel at that age. They got
this cold wind called indifference. *(Beat.)* I have seen
things, people dying in the streets, people dying of disease
invented in my own lifetime. When I was a kid, Nicky
Whit and I went to Tijuana and we saw people begging
for change and living in the streets hungry. And Nicky
Whit said, "We're American. You won't see that in America." Well, he was wrong.

ED: Well, what do you expect from a guy named Nit Whitt.

RICK: Now, I have to finish this story. People like happy endings. I just can't find one.

ED: Maybe I'll get well. I could place in the Senior Olympics.

RICK: That's a good ending.

ED: I could win the super Lotto. I'm Mexican. The general
public will believe it.

RICK: I need an even happier ending.

ED: Sometimes, there isn't supposed to be a happy ending.
There's many kinds of endings. I was so happy the day I
got married. I thought, wow, this is my happy ending. I
wish I could die now. But I would have missed you being
born or teaching Clint how to sail or Cherie's wedding. Or
taking her to watch "Camelot." Did they turn you down in
Hollywood?

RICK: Yeah. I went through a riot, lost the woman I loved,
and my apartment got destroyed in an earthquake. I lost
my job, my friends. Then things started to get really bad.
I can't point to five kids. I can't point to a war won. I can't
point to anything you can.

ED: You have done great things.

RICK: I recorded a life; you have lived it. I'm tired, Dad.

ED: You're getting closer to that one "yes," that's all. You got
to see that.

RICK: I get to see that all I have written will be shadows
after you go.

ED: Well, I love having you around, but you got to get back to L.A. and work.

RICK: What work?

ED: You know why your great-grandfather actually came to this country? To work. I thought that reason was too boring for your story. He came here to work, and that's what we do.

RICK: But there isn't any work! I've been shut out. I've got no job, other than a commission for this play, and that's it.

ED: Well, if there isn't a job, it's your job to create one; 'cause you're an artist. Right? An artist creates; you create beginnings and endings with words. I love words. You can put them in any hundreds of various combinations and they mean something different. That's why I loved Toastmasters.

RICK: Dad, I don't even have any endings for this story. I'm scared of where this ending is headed.

ED: Well, there doesn't have to be a happy ending. Just tell the truth. Tell the truth. Now, I got to rest a little. *(He starts to leave, then turns.)*

ED: Rick, I want you to remember, every time you get a "no," you are getting closer to a "yes." It's mathematics. Get out there! Go door to door, knocking, and look for opportunity. If you don't have hope, well, you can borrow some of mine. I'll put it in my will along with my camera. *(Ed starts to sit down.)* God damn, my body is betraying me. I feel weak. I can't eat food. I drink shakes. I envy everything you got. *(Rick sits down also.)*

ED: Why are you sitting down?

RICK: I thought it was rude to be standing when you're collapsing.

ED: Is there some sort of collapsing etiquette?

RICK: I don't know.

ED: Well, I'll tell you. I want you to stand, especially if I fall. What kind of story are you going to write? *(Mary enters the room.)*

MARY: What are you doing up? Eddie, you've got to rest. I've been praying for you. I have a whole order of monks praying for you. Those prayed for are more likely to get well. Now, get in bed. Prayers will have to work extra hard if you don't help.

ED: Did you tell the monks to pray for my left side? I bet you didn't. Mary, pray me to my room.

RICK: Dad, I'll help you. *(Rick starts to help him to his room.)*

ED: When you were little I went to kiss you and you said, "Dad, I'm a big boy now." So I never hugged and kissed you again.

RICK: You should have never listened to a kid, Dad. *(Ed hugs Rick.)*

ED: Your mother will take me to my room. I want to hear you writing away. That's what you do. That is your job, your work. *(Mary starts to walk out with Ed. Ed gives Rick the trench coat again.)* Wear this coat. It's yours. It'll keep you warm. I expect you to be going to L.A. in the morning.

RICK: Yeah. Thanks for the coat.

MARY: Is the play you're writing about the war?

RICK: No, Mom, it's going to be a love story.

MARY: *(Smiles.)* Oh good, love stories are so much nicer.
(Ed grabs Rick.)

ED: I want you writing.

RICK: I'll put you to bed. I'll write later.

ED: Does it get cold in L.A? *(Mary watches Ed and Rick walk away.)*

RICK: Yeah, Dad, it gets cold in L.A.

MARY: *(Walks to the middle of the stage and looks at papers and a tape recorder. She picks up the tape recorder. The lights change into darkness around a simple pool of light where Mary stands. She looks at the audience and the sunset and speaks into the tape recorder.)* Rick, I went to the Indian reservation to play the slots after your father left. *(Beat.)* He left us in the morning. Almost as if he was going to work, like he did every day for twenty-five years at North Island. He raised his hands out towards heaven and he was gone. He flew away like that bird he raised once. Well, he left. Where was I? I was at the Casino. And you know what? I was losing and I had my last dollar and I looked up and said, "Eddy, you're not doing any-thing in heaven. Why don't you help me?" *(Her speech turns into a taped conversation. She stands there. The tape runs out just as her speech ends. The effect is as if she has become one of the conversations taped during the play. The effect should be as if she fades with the tape recording, lights and sound together.)* And you know what? Right then I pulled the lever and I won six hundred and fifty dollars. Thank you, Eddy. Hey Eddy, isn't it ironic? I did get the last word, after all.

BLACK OUT.

Corrido plays "A Quiet Love," *"Un amor Callado."*

FADE OUT.